Snorkel Maui

Lāna'i and Moloka'i

Guide to the Beaches and Snorkeling of Hawai'i • Judy & Mel Malinowski

Snorkel Maui Lanai and Molokai
Guide to the Beaches and Snorkeling of Hawaii

Third Edition © 2008 by Judy and Mel Malinowski

Published by: Indigo Publications
       e-mail: indigo@snorkelguides.com

SAN 298-9921
Publisher's symbol: Indigo CA

Printed in China by C & C Offset Printing Co., Inc.

All landscape photography ©Mel Malinowski.
All underwater photography ©Jay Torborg unless otherwise noted.

Award-winning photographer Jay Torborg has been photographing nature for almost 30 years. Jay started out focusing on landscape photography, but over the last several years, his photographic interests have shifted toward wildlife and underwater photography. More of Jay's photography can be seen on his web site: www. torborgphoto.com.

Jay uses Nikon D1X professional digital SLRs with a wide range of professional Nikon lenses for most of his photography. For underwater photography, he uses this same camera mounted in a Seacam housing with two Ikelite 200 strobes.

About the cover: Hawai'ian day octopus photo by Jay Torborg.

Thanks to the many kind-spirited people of Hawai'i who bring the spirit of aloha to all they do. Special thanks to Dr. John Randall and John Hoover for their inspirational and detail-rich reference books on the sea life of our islands, and helpful counsel. Thanks to Danny Akaka for advising and teaching us by his example. Through him, we have come to better understand the beauty and value of Hawai'ian language and culture.

ISBN 9780964668089

Library of Congress Control Number: 2008900160

Contents

Orientation
4   Maui Road Map
6   Why Snorkel Maui?

Ready
8   Basics
9   Gear Selection
18   Into the Water
24   Caring for Your Gear
26   Hazards

Sites
36   Where are Those Fish?
38   Maui Site Index Map
40   Maui Sites at a Glance
44   North
60   West
82   Lahaina
90   Olowalu
100   Kīhei
110   Wailea
134   South
158   East
174   Lāna'i Site Index Map
176   Lāna'i Sites at a Glance
178   Lāna'i
192   Moloka'i

Useful Information
196   Marine Life
210   Weather
214   Language
216   Often Heard Myths

Reference
218   Index
224   About the Authors

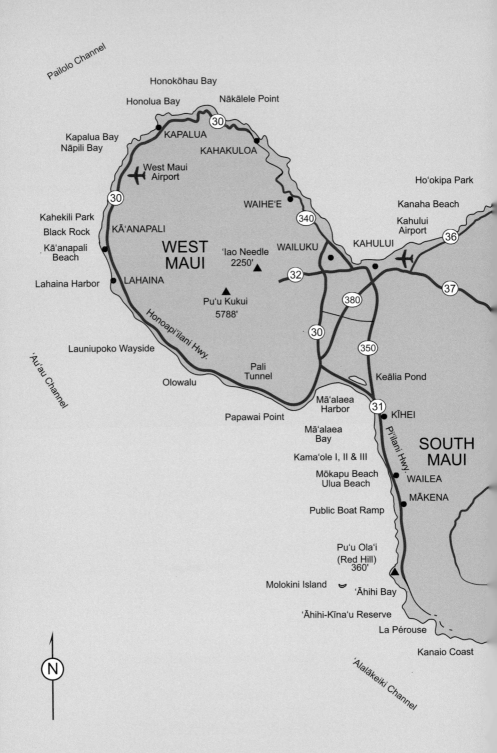

Pailolo Channel

Honokōhau Bay

Honolua Bay   Nākālele Point

Kapalua Bay   (30)
Nāpili Bay   KAPALUA

KAHAKULOA

West Maui   Ho'okipa Park
Airport

Kahekili Park   WAIHE'E   Kanaha Beach
Black Rock   KĀ'ANAPALI   (340)   Kahului
Kā'anapali   WEST   Airport
Beach   MAUI   WAILUKU   KAHULUI   (36)
'Iao Needle
Lahaina Harbor   LAHAINA   2250'
(32)
(37)
Pu'u Kukui
5788'   (380)

Honoapi'ilani Hwy.

Launiupoko Wayside   (30)

'Au'au Channel   Pali   (350)
Tunnel   Keālia Pond
Olowalu

Mā'alaea   (31)
Papawai Point   Harbor   KĪHEI

Mā'alaea
Bay   SOUTH
Kama'ole I, II & III   MAUI

Mōkapu Beach   P'iilani Hwy.
Ulua Beach   WAILEA

Public Boat Ramp   MĀKENA

Pu'u Ola'i
(Red Hill)
360'
Molokini Island   'Āhihi Bay

'Āhihi-Kīna'u Reserve
La Pérouse

Kanaio Coast

'Alalākeiki Channel

N

4

Maui Road Map

(Also see Snorkeling Site
Index Map on page 38)

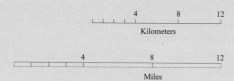

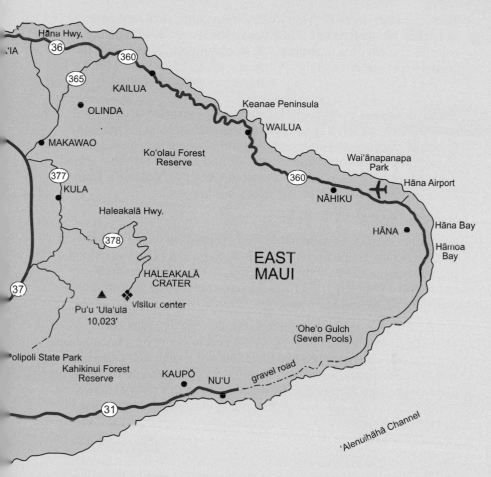

Hāna Hwy.

36

'IA

360

365

KAILUA

OLINDA

MAKAWAO

Keanae Peninsula

WAILUA

Ko'olau Forest
Reserve

Wai'ānapanapa
Park

377

360

Hāna Airport

KULA

NĀHIKU

Haleakalā Hwy.

HĀNA

Hāna Bay

378

Hāmoa
Bay

EAST
MAUI

HALEAKALĀ
CRATER

37

vIsitor center

Pu'u 'Ula'ula
10,023'

'Ohe'o Gulch
(Seven Pools)

olipoli State Park

Kahikinui Forest
Reserve

KAUPŌ

NU'U

gravel road

31

'Alenuihāhā Channel

5

Why Snorkel Maui?

Maui and Lāna'i offer more snorkeling sites within easy reach than any other Hawai'ian island. There is something here for every snorkeler and ample variety to keep a whole family happy. Laze around on endless golden beaches and cool yourself with colorful snorkeling swims. Follow this up with good food, shopping and socializing if you're so inclined. It's all close at hand on Maui.

There are many sites with easy entry from calm, sheltered bays and broad, sandy beaches. Maui has extensive reefs with plenty of colorful and exciting creatures. Popular Molokini Island, with its crystal-clear waters, and the unique islands of Lāna'i and Moloka'i lie just a brief excursion away, and offer a change of pace.

The choices are ample: beautiful, sweeping expanses of soft coral sand and diverse snorkeling sites; action-packed total destination resorts with every amenity; secluded little-known beach retreats just around the bend; or nearby, less-visited pristine neighbor island hideaways along the southern shores of Lāna'i or Moloka'i. Choices like this have made Maui a legendary destination.

Snorkel Maui and Lāna'i makes it easy

An active vacation is memorable for adventure as well as relaxation. Hassles and missteps finding out where to go can raise your blood pressure and waste your time. We've done extensive research that will help you quickly locate appropriate sites that fit your interests and abilities, saving your valuable vacation hours.

Snorkeling sites in Hawai'i are sometimes tricky because of changeable waves and currents, so it's best to get good advice before heading out. Everyone has had their share of unpleasant experiences due to vague directions as well as outdated or inaccurate information. We have created the Snorkel Hawai'i series as that savvy snorkeling buddy everyone needs. Many personal stories help bring the sea life of Hawai'i more alive for our readers. See About the Authors on page 224 if you want to know a little more about us.

We have snorkeled all the sites listed, including many that are not well known. The challenge lies in finding them quickly, as well as how to enter and exit, and where to snorkel, so you'll have a safe and rewarding experience. Our detailed maps, instructions and pictures will ease the uncertainty, saving you time and effort. Try to visit Maui, Lāna'i and Moloka'i at least once in your life and by all means experience the underwater world. Aloha!

—Judy and Mel Malinowski

Snorkeling is...

- easy

- relaxing

- fun

- floating on the surface of the sea

- breathing without effort through a tube

- peering into the water world through a mask

- open to any age, size, shape or ability

Who was the first snorkeler? As the fossil records include few petrified snorkels, we are free to speculate.

Among larger creatures, elephants are the pioneers and current champions, as they have known how to snorkel for countless generations. Once in a blue moon, you may see a elephant herd heading out to do lunch on an island off the coast of Tanzania, paddling along with their trunks held high. No one knows whether the hefty pachyderms enjoy the fish-watching, but you can bet a big liquid chuckle reverberates through the ranks of reef fish in the vicinity as the parade goes by.

As evolution continued, perhaps a clever member of the promising Homo sapiens species saved his furry brow by hiding underwater from pursuers, breathing through a hollow reed. Masks came much later, so the fish probably looked a little fuzzy. Surviving to propagate his brainy kind, he founded a dynasty of snorkelers. Perhaps he actually liked the peaceful atmosphere down there, and a new sport was born.

Some of our readers may grumble that snorkeling is not a real sport: no rules, no score, no competition, scarcely aerobic, with hardly any equipment or clothing. We say to them: lighten up, you're on vacation!! Relax in the water—go for a long run later.

Incorrigible competitors can create their own competition by counting how many species they've seen or trying to spot the biggest or the most seen in one day. Everybody else can ease into the welcoming waters of Hawai'i and just have fun being a part of nature's colorful, salty, wet, ancient home.

Basics

To snorkel you need only two things:

Snorkel — Saves lifting your head once a minute, wasting energy and disturbing the fish.

Mask — While you can see (poorly) without one, it keeps the water out of your eyes and lets you see clearly.

Rent them inexpensively at many local shops or buy them if you prefer. It's all the back-to-basics folks need to snorkel in calm warm water, where there aren't any currents or hazards.

Savvy snorkelers often add a few items to the list, based on years of experience, such as:

Swimsuit — Required by law in many localities. Added benefit: saves you from an occasional all-body sunburn.

Fins — Good if you want to swim with ease and speed like a fish. Saves energy. A must in Hawai'i, due to occasional strong currents. They protect your tender feet too.

T-shirt — Simple way to avoid or minimize sunburn on your back. Available everywhere in many colors.

Sunscreen — Save sunscreen for after your snorkel to avoid getting it into your eyes and polluting the reef area. Use a lycra skin instead.

Lycra Skin — A great all-body cover-up for warm weather. Provides much better protection than a T-shirt, and saves gallons of sunscreen. Keeps you from leaving a sunscreen oil slick in your wake. Available in most dive shops, and a good investment.

Wetsuit — For some, the Hawai'ian waters seem a bit chilly, not exactly pool-warm. Wetsuits range from simple T-shirt-like tops to full suits. Worth considering. Fringe benefit: sun protection!

You're almost ready to get wet. But wait! You want to know even more technical detail? Every sport has an equipment list—it's what keeps sporting goods stores in business and your garage shelves full.

Gear Selection

Good snorkeling gear enables you to pay attention to the fish instead of uncomfortable distractions. Poor equipment will make you suffer in little ways, from pressure headaches caused by a too-tight mask, to blisters on your feet from ill-fitting fins. Consider your alternatives carefully before buying and you'll have more fun later. This is a case of "pain, no gain." If it hurts, fix it, and you'll be glad you did. You may want to rent & try gear first. See page 145 for tips about renting.

Snorkel

Snorkels can be quite cheap. Be prepared to pony up $25 or more, however, if you want them to last longer and be more comfortable. You'll appreciate a comfortable mouthpiece if you plan to snorkel for long. Watch out for hard edges—a good mouthpiece is smooth and chewy-soft. Some of the more expensive mouthpieces swivel for comfort. We like that better than corrugated models.

Several new high-tech models have been designed to minimize water coming down the tube from chop or an occasional swell overtopping you. We looked at these with mild skepticism until a choppy snorkeling trip had us coughing and clearing our snorkels every third breath. With our new dry snorkels, that water never makes it to the mouthpiece.

Technology continues to advance, so you can now get a snorkel that will keep ALL of the water out, even if you dive beneath the surface. Don't ask us how they do it, but it works well! Even in very choppy conditions, you never worry about water coming in. We like dry snorkels, at about $40 and up. They certainly make learning to snorkel as easy as possible, although they are not a necessity.

These fancier snorkels do need care because you won't want a valve to fail just as you arrive at that perfect destination. Keep them out of the sand! Repairs or replacements are available at most dive shops.

Snorkel Holder

This little guy holds your snorkel to your mask strap, so you don't keep dipping it in the sea. The old standard is a simple figure 8 double loop that pulls over the snorkel tube, wraps around your mask strap, and then back over the tube. A hefty rubber band will work passably in a pinch. The downside of this type of snorkel holder is that it doesn't slide up and down easily, and often gets tangled with long hair. The good news is that there is a better way available. The higher end snorkels often have a slot or movable ring that allows the snorkel to be adjusted easily. It slides easily rather than having to be tugged. The standard scuba snorkel position is on your left side. You might as well get used to it there since you may dive eventually.

Mask

Nothing can color your snorkeling experience more than an ill-fitting mask (unless, of course, you get that all-body sunburn mentioned earlier). Don't settle for painful or leaky masks! If it hurts, it's not your problem—it's the mask that's wrong for you. Remember our snorkeling principle: "pain, no gain"!

Simple variety store masks can cost as little as $10. Top-quality masks from a dive shop run upwards of $60. Consider starting out with a rental mask, paying a bit extra for the better quality models. As you gain more experience, you'll be in a better position to evaluate a mask before you lock yourself into one style.

You need a good fit to your particular facial geometry. Shops often tell you to place the mask on your face (without the strap) and breathe in. If the mask will stay in place, then they say you have found a good fit. However, nearly all masks will stay on my face under this test, yet some leak later! You can do better.

Look for soft edges and a mask that conforms to your face even before drawing in your breath. There's a great deal of variance in where a mask rests on your face and how soft it feels, so compare very carefully. Look for soft and comfortable, unless you especially like having pressure headaches and don't mind looking like a very large octopus glommed on to your face.

Lack of 20-20 vision needn't cut into your viewing pleasure, but it does require a little more effort during equipment selection. Those who wear contact lenses can use them within their masks, taking on the risk that they'll swish out and float softly and invisibly down to the sea bed, perhaps to be found by a fossil hunter in the distant future, but certainly not by you. Use the disposable kind. Unless you use contacts, search for a correctable mask. Vision-correcting lens are available for many masks in 1/2 diopter increments.

If the mask you prefer doesn't offer standard correcting lenses, custom prescription lenses can be fitted to almost any mask.

Moorish idol

This costs more and takes longer. Even bifocals are available. We happen to prefer the comfortable prescription masks made by SeaVision which can be ordered with any custom correction. The cost is much like normal prescription lenses.

Mustaches create a mask leakage problem. As Mel likes the look of a mustache, he has coped with this his entire adult life. Some advise the use petroleum jelly or silicon compound to make a more effective seal. That doesn't appeal to him since he goes in and out of the water several times a day. It does help to choose a mask that rests high over the mouth and perhaps trim the top 1/8 inch or so off the center mustache, if it sticks up. Hair breaks the seal and allows water to seep into the mask slowly, so you'll still have to clear the mask occasionally. Mel tolerated half an inch of water in the bottom of his mask for years, until he got a good purge valve mask. Much better!

His Sea Vision mask mounts a purge valve in the bottom of the nosepiece. If some water leaks in, he just lightly blows a little air out the nose, taking the water with it. This is much easier and more effective than lifting the bottom of the mask to blow the water out.

The conventional wisdom in scuba is that purge valves are an unnecessary weak point. So far, we haven't had any trouble with ours. Some experienced divers do use them and swear by them. This isn't an issue snorkelers need worry about. If you find a purge valve mask that fits well, use it for snorkeling. You'll be glad you did!

11

Mask Strap

The rubber strap that comes with the mask can tangle your hair. If you have your own mask and want it to slide on more easily, there's a comfortable strap available with velcro adjustment. The back is made of wetsuit material—stretchy and soft. Cost is about $10-15 in dive shops. Since we get in and out often, we happen to prefer this one, but it's a convenience for the frequent snorkeler rather than a necessity and it doesn't dry fast.

Fins

The simplest fins are basic (usually black) enclosed foot fins. These are one-piece molded rubber and slip right on to your bare feet. For basic snorkeling, these inexpensive fins are fine. We own several kinds of fins and still sometimes choose the one-piece foot fins for lightness and compact packing. They seem to last forever and are inexpensive ($15-$25). Mel has had to shave off the sharp edge just under where your toes go, as it sticks up too far and rubs. This is easy to do with a carpet knife.

Why should anyone look further? Because it is possible to get better comfort and more thrust. Specialized fins are now made for higher performance and can run $100 or more.

Long stiff fins are excellent for surface diving and speed, but can be tiring and cause muscle cramps if you're not an athlete.

Scuba divers often use strap-on fins with wetsuit booties. They're available in lots of colors and styles, but float your feet too high for efficient snorkeling. Soft, split blade fins are our current favorites because they are comfortable and less tiring when snorkeling long distance or through rough water. Oceanic Vortex are particularly comfortable if you have a narrow foot. While they may seem too soft for speed, we find them excellent for our snorkeling.

If you're inclined to get blisters, pay more attention to softness and fit. Liners are available, but usually not necessary. Blisters are NOT inevitable, so some people may need to keep hunting for the best fins for the shape of untypical feet. Unless it's absolutely certain that no current can carry you away,

ALWAYS WEAR FINS!

As you look at more advanced fins, they split into two attachment methods with pros and cons to each type. We own both and pick the best for a particular situation.

ENCLOSED FOOT	Your bare foot slides into a stretchy, integral molded rubber shoe.
Advantages	The lightest, most streamlined and fish-like fit. It probably is the most efficient at transmitting your muscle power to the blade. We prefer this type when booties are not required for warmth or safety. We find that we almost always choose and wear this kind.
Disadvantages	The fins must be closely fitted to your particular foot size and shape. Some models may cause blisters. You need to find a brand that fits the shape of your foot well. If you have to hike in to the entry site, you need separate shoes. This may preclude entering at one spot, and exiting elsewhere. If the entry is over sharp coral or other hazards, these may not be the best choice. But you really shouldn't be walking on the coral anyway.
STRAP-ON	Made for use with booties.
Advantages	Makes rough surface entry easy. Just hike to the entry point, head on into the water holding your fins in hand, and lay back to pull on your fins. Exiting is just as easy. The bootie cushions your foot, making blisters unlikely. Widely used for scuba.
Disadvantages	Less streamlined. The bootie makes your feet float up, so you may have trouble keeping your fins from breaking the surface.

No matter how good the fins, snorkeling for long hours may cause blisters—especially on the heel. No need to worry if you carry 3M Nexcare waterproof bandages. These little essentials will do the job and stay in place well when wet. Buy them at any major pharmacy.

Reef Shoes or Booties

Walking with bare feet on ʻaʻa (sharp lava) or coral can shred your feet in a quick minute. There are fine reef shoes available that are happy in or out of the water. These are primarily for getting there, or wading around, as they don't really work that well with strap-on fins.

For the sake of the reef, don't actually walk on a reef with reef shoes, since each step kills hundreds of the little animals that make up the living reef.

Zip-on booties are widely used by divers and allow use of strap-on fins. They do float your feet—a disadvantage for snorkelers.

Keeping Time

One easy-to-forget item: a water-resistant watch. This needn't be expensive and is very useful for pacing yourself and keeping track of your sun exposure time.

"Water resistant" alone usually means that a little rain won't wreck the watch, but immersion in water may. When a designation like "to 10 meters" is added, it denotes added water-resistance; but the dynamic pressures from swimming increase the pressure, so choose 50 meters or greater rating to be safe even when snorkeling. Don't take a 50 meter watch scuba diving, though—that requires 100-200 meter models.

Hawaiʻian time is two hours earlier than Pacific Standard Time (winter) or three hours earlier than Pacific Daylight Time. Hawaiʻi doesn't observe Daylight Savings Time.

Body Suit

There are a variety of all-body suits that protect you from sun exposure and light abrasion, but provide no warmth. They are made from various synthetic fabrics—lycra and nylon being common. They cost much less than wetsuits and are light and easy to pack.

We usually bring ours along as a sun protection alternative in warmer conditions. If you don't want to look like a F.O.B. (Fresh Off the Boat) tourist, with a shocking pink outline of your swimsuit, plan ahead about sun protection. You'll sleep better if you do. The coral and fish will not miss all that sunscreen fouling their water. And you'll be able to snorkel longer, in the middle of the day if you want, without the risk of that trip-ruining painful sunburn.

14

Wetsuit

In Maui, water temperature on the surface varies from a low of about 75° F in March to a high of about 80° F in September. If you happen to be slender, no longer young or from a moderate climate, this can seem cold. Sheltered bays and tidepools can be a bit warmer while deeper water can be surprisingly cold. Fresh water runoff can also make water cooler than you might expect. We've snorkeled in March when we swore it was not a bit warmer than 65° off Kaua'i. Maybe not, but even two degrees cooler feels like six or eight!

Regardless of the exact temperature, the water is cooler than your body. With normal exertion, your body still cools bit by bit. After awhile, perhaps 30-45 minutes, you start feeling a little chilly. Later you begin shivering and eventually hypothermia begins.

We often snorkel for more than an hour. A thin, 3mm full wetsuit protects us from the sun while keeping us warm and comfortable in the summer and fall. Some folks don't need this in warmer weather. Others like us have little natural padding, get cold easily. In the cooler winter and spring water, we either add a "core warmer" on top of our 3mm suits, or switch to a 5mm full wetsuit.

Off the rack suits are a bargain and fit most folks. Look for a snug fit at neck, wrists and ankles—if your suit is loose there, water will flow in and out, making you cold. If you have big feet and small ankles, get zippers on the legs if possible or you'll really have to struggle to remove the suit when it's wet.

Wetsuit wearers also get added range and buoyancy, and they hardly need a life jacket! Wearing a wetsuit, you can stay in the water without hypothermia for many hours   even in the winter. This could be comforting in the unlikely event that some strong current sweeps you off towards Fiji. There are few situations from which you can't rescue yourself if you're wearing a wetsuit and fins.

We've found a wetsuit favorite brand, Henderson Wetsuits from New Jersey. We like their variety of wetsuits for different purposes. Our favorite model is called "Hyperstretch Titanium", because the superstretchability of the fabric makes it easy to get on and off, it adapts to various body shapes, and flexes with you as you swim. It is unquestionably the most comfortable wetsuit we own. However, we have noticed that it is not quite as warm for a given thickness as some of their other models. The three millimeter-thick version is light, and warm enough for Hawai'i summer and fall snorkeling. Thicker versions that are warmer are also available. Other types include Gold Core (easier to slide on and off) and Instadry, which scarcely absorbs water. Instadry is stiffer and stickier than the other models, but it has an important advantage: you can shake the water off it, and little water is left. This is great for repetitive snorkeling from a boat, or travel. It has become our travel favorite.

Henderson has been promoting layered systems. The idea is to wear a thin full wetsuit, and then add a core warmer on top, which is like a shorty, but without sleeves. We've come around to liking this system, as it allows you to easily adjust the warmth to the conditions.

Dave Barry once described putting on a wetsuit as like wrestling with an octopus. Not this one! No more hanging onto the shower while your buddy tries to pull the wetsuit off your ankles with a winch. If you can afford the extra cost, these suits are superb. We had ours custom-made with longer arms and legs, and no rubberized kneepads. We like our wetsuits sleek and flexible, and we never wear out the knees. Divers who kneel a lot may need knee pads.

Swim Cap

If you have trouble with long hair tangling in your mask straps while snorkeling, get a lycra Speedo swim cap. It may look silly, but it works, and also protects your scalp from too many rays.

Snorkeling Vest

It is possible to buy inflatable vests made for snorkeling. Some guidebooks and stores promote them as virtually essential. We've taken excursions that require all snorkelers to wear one. Other excursions encourage the use of flotation noodles or kick boards—whatever it takes to make you comfortable.

Vests are hardly necessary in salt water for most people, but can be useful if you can't swim a lick or won't be willing to try this sport without it. There is a possible safety edge for kids or older folks. If you do get a vest, you can give it to another beginner after you get used to snorkeling. You will discover that it takes little effort to float flat in salt water while breathing through a snorkel.

If you feel you need extra flotation, consider using a light wetsuit instead of a life vest. It simultaneously gives you buoyancy, sun and critter protection, as well as warmth.

Low Volume Masks

When you begin looking at masks, the variety can be bewildering. How can you figure out which design is best for you?

Inexpensive masks often have one large flat front glass. They're OK if the skirt of the mask fits you, although they're often a bit stiff and uncomfortable. They also tend to be far out from your face with a big air space. As you go up in price, the lenses tend to get smaller and closer to your eyes, as preferred by divers.

There is a good scuba reason for this. These are called low volume masks. They contain less airspace and so require less effort to clear when water gets in. They also press less against your face when you go deeper and the pressure rises (if you forget to blow higher pressure air in through your nose) and hence are more comfortable when diving.

For a snorkeler this is of little importance, but it still should be considered as you select your mask. Many snorkelers go on to do some surface diving, as well as Snuba or scuba diving. When you dive down even 10 feet, the water pressure is considerable. At 32 feet, the air in your lungs and mask is compressed to half its volume. Unless you blow some air into your mask through your nose, the pressure on your face can be quite uncomfortable!

If your mask is flooded, which does happen, it is easier to clear out a low volume mask. So, while it's not the most important factor, if everything else is equal, low volume is better.

Surface Diving Gear

For surface diving, bigger fins improve your range. Those surreal-looking Cressi fins that seem about three feet long will take you down so fast you'll be amazed. You'll also be amazed how few suitcases are big enough to accommodate them, and how inadequate your legs feel to kick them for an hour, unless you're very athletic.

A long-fin alternative is to use a soft weight belt with from 2 to 4 pounds (more if you wear a wetsuit)—just enough to help you get under the surface without using up all your energy. As you descend, you become neutrally buoyant at about 15-20 feet so you don't have to fight popping up. Of course, the sword cuts two ways, since you must swim up under your own power in time to breathe.

Into the Water

Getting Started

Now that you've assembled a nice collection of snorkel gear, you're ready to go! On a sunny tropical morning you're down at the water's edge. Little one-foot waves slap the sand lightly, while a soft warm breeze takes the edge off the intensity of the climbing sun. It's a great day to be alive and out in the water.

Going snorkeling, it's better to have no suntan lotion on your face or hands. You sure don't want it washing into your eyes to make them burn and water. Wear a nice big hat instead on your way to the water. You applied lotion to your back before you left, so it had time to become effective. Then you washed off your hands and rinsed them well so the lotion couldn't contaminate your mask later.

Or you could do like we do, and skip all the lotion. Being outside as much as we are, and in and out of the water, we prefer to carefully cover up instead—we find too much lotion hard on our skin. Big broad hats like your boat captain wears help. Comfortable cotton cover-ups look good and are cool. Lycra body suits or wetsuits in the water let you stay in for as long as you wish. Do watch out for reflected light on long boat trips, which can sneak in and sizzle your tender face.

convict tang

Checking Conditions

Take it nice and slow. Sit down and watch the waves for awhile. Check the slope of the beach. Consider whether there might be currents. Look for wave patterns, how big the biggest waves are and how far they wash up on the beach. When you see the pattern, you're ready to go. Set your gear down back well beyond the furthest watermarks on the sand. You don't want that seventh wave to sweep your gear away! Watch as long as it takes to be sure conditions aren't changing for the worse.

Gearing Up

Now defog the mask so that water vapor from your nose, or water leakage, won't bead up on your mask lens and spoil your view. There are several ways to defog that work well.

The classic solution is: SPIT. Spit on the inside of your dry mask lens, and rub it all around with your sunscreen-free finger. Step into the water, just out beyond the stirred up sand, and dip up a mask full of clear saltwater. Thoroughly rub and rinse off that spit, and dump the mask. Now you have prepared a mask that may be fog-resistant for the length of an average snorkel.

If you spit and polish, and still have fogging problems, there are several possible causes. Your mask may be gooped up with cosmetics, dried on saltwater residue or whatever other goo may be out there. A good cleaning with toothpaste may be in order (see Caring for Your Gear, page 24).

It's possible that you didn't actually wet all the surface with spit—perhaps because there were drops of water left on the lens. In that case, or if you just feel funny about spitting in your mask, you can use no-fog solution. It actually does work even better than spit. No-fog comes in small, handy, inexpensive bottles that seem to last forever because you use only a few drops at a time.

If you prefer to make your own, a mixture of half baby shampoo (so you don't irritate your eyes) and half water works fine. Some recipes add alcohol to the mix. Unless you are an excursion boat operator and use defog by the gallon, it's easier to just buy some!

Our favorite trick is to pre-apply no-fog solution to the dry masks as we load up our gear, and then let it dry. When you get to the water, just rinse out the mask thoroughly. This seems to last a long time.

Getting Comfortable

After you rinse your mask, try its fit. Adjust the mask strap and snorkel until they're comfortable. Hold the snorkel in your mouth without tightening your jaws. It can be quite loose without falling out. Putting your mask on long before you enter the water can cause it to fog from your exertions.

Getting Wet

Now retrieve your fins and walk back in the water, watching the waves carefully. NEVER turn your back on the ocean for long, lest a rogue wave sneak up on you and whack you good. The key is to stay alert and awake—especially on entry and exit.

If the bottom is sandy smooth, wade on out until you're about waist deep. Pull your mask on, making sure you remove any stray hair from under the edge. Position the snorkel in your mouth and start breathing. You can practice this in a pool or hot tub.

Duck down in the water so you're floating and pull on your fins just like sneakers. Be sure no sand is trapped in the fins. Make a smooth roll to your stomach, pause to float and relax until you're comfortable, and you're off! Flip those fins and you have begun your re-entry into the sea.

As you float, practice steady breathing through the snorkel. Breathe slowly and deeply. People sometimes tense up at first and take short breaths. When this happens, you're only getting stale air from the snorkel rather than lots of fresh air from outside. If you ever feel tired or out of breath, don't remove your mask. Just stop as long as necessary, float, breathe easy and relax.

After you've become quite comfortable breathing this way, check how your mask is doing. Make sure it isn't leaking. Adjust the strap if needed. And keep adjusting until it's just right. Slide your snorkel strap to a comfortable position, with the tube pointing about straight up as you float looking down at about a 30° angle.

Swimming while snorkeling is easy once you've relaxed. No arms are required. What works best is to hold your arms straight back along your sides, keep your legs fairly straight and kick those fins slowly without bending your knees much. Any swimming technique will work, of course, but some are more tiring. Practice using the least amount of energy. Once you learn how to snorkel the easy way,

Motion Sickness

Motion sickness (such as seasickness, carsickness or airsickness) is a minor inner ear disorder which can really cut into your pleasure on the water, on long, curvy road trips or in choppy air. Fortunately, motion sickness is quite controllable these days. All it takes is a little advance planning to turn a potentially miserable experience into a normal, fun one. Don't let old fears keep you from great water adventures anymore.

Mel can get seasick just by vividly imagining a rocking boat, so he has personally tried just about every remedy. These field trials are a messy business, so we'll spare you the details, and just pass on what really works in our experience.

Forget the wrist pressure-point bands—they don't do the job for anyone we've ever met. You might as well put them in the closet along with your ultrasonic pest repeller, in our opinion.

The most effective remedy we've found so far is Meclizine, a pill formerly available by prescription, but now over the counter. It works perfectly for Mel with no noticeable side effects. Alcohol can apparently interact with it to make you drowsy, though Mel has had a beer on excursions without falling asleep.

We learned about Meclizine when Jon Carroll, a columnist in the San Francisco Chronicle, reported that it had sufficed for him in 15-25 foot swells on the way to Antarctica. If it does the job there, it should handle all but the most radical of snorkeling excursions. It's always worked for us.

An over-the-counter alternative is Benadryl usually used as a decongestant. It can also be effective against motion sickness. Ginger is also claimed to be effective. As much as we enjoy ginger as a spice, we cannot substantiate that it helps at all.

Use these medicines carefully and only after consulting your doctor. In some cases, you must avoid alcohol, other drugs or diving, since these medications can produce drowsiness.

you can use all the power you like touring large areas as if you were a migrating whale. But if you're breaking the surface with your fins, going "splash, plunk, splash", you're wasting energy. Be cool and smooth and quiet as a fish, and you'll swim like a dolphin.

eyestripe surgeonfish

Clearing Your Mask

Eventually you will need to practice clearing your mask. If you
have a purge valve, just blow out gently. The scuba method: take
a deep breath, then tip your head up, but with the mask still under
the surface. Press your palm to the top of the mask against your
forehead, or hold your fingers on the top of the mask and exhale
through your nose. This forces water out the bottom of the mask.

Taking It Easy

Relax and try not to push yourself too hard. Experienced snorkelers
may urge you on faster than you're comfortable because they've
forgotten how it feels to get started. As your experience builds, you'll
find it easy too. It's like learning to drive a car. Remember how
even a parking lot seemed like a challenge? It helps to practice your
beginning snorkeling in a calm easy place—with a patient teacher.
With a little persistence, you'll soon overcome your fears and be
ready. Don't feel like you should rush. Play around and have fun!

Pacing

When you're having a good time, it's easy to forget and over-extend yourself. That next rocky point beckons, and then a pretty spot beyond that. Pretty soon, you're many miles from home and getting tired. Getting cold and overly tired can contribute to poor judgement in critical situations, making you more vulnerable to injury. Why risk turning your great snorkeling experience into a disaster? Learn your limits, and how to pace yourself.

Our favorite technique: If we plan on a one-hour snorkel, we watch the time and start heading back when we've been in the water 30 minutes. If the currents could run against us on the way back, we allow extra time and energy. We like to start our snorkel by swimming against the current, making the trip home surprisingly easy and quick.

If you're cruising along, making great time, pay extra attention. Rather than being a snorkeling superman all of a sudden, you may be drifting along with a fast current. Stop and check the drift by watching the coral below you, and plankton in the water. If there is a current, allow extra time/energy for swimming back against it. Or if you're towing your reef shoes along, sometimes you can enjoy the ride and walk back (assuming you're sure there's a good exit ahead). You can use your fins for shade.

Knowing Your Limits

Have you heard the old saloon saying: "Don't let your mouth write checks that your body can't cover"?

Let's paraphrase this as "Don't let your ego take you places your body can't get you back from." Consider carefully how well-conditioned your legs are, so you'll have enough reserve to be able to make it back home, and then some in case of an emergency.

Snorkeling Alone

In your enthusiasm for the reef, you may wind up in this situation: your significant other prefers watching sports on ESPN to snorkeling one afternoon, and you're sorely tempted to just head out there alone. Think twice. Snorkeling, done in buddy teams, is a pretty safe recreation, especially if conditions are favorable. Just as in scuba diving, having a buddy along reduces the risk of a small problem becoming a big problem or even a fatal problem. We won't spell out all the bad things that could happen; we trust your imagination.

23

Caring for Your Gear

You just had a great snorkeling experience—now you can thank the gear that helped make it possible, by taking good care of it.

Rinse and Dry

If there are beach showers, head right up and rinse off. Salt residue is sticky and corrosive. Rinse salt and sand off your wetsuit, fins, mask and snorkel before the saltwater dries. If you can, dry your gear in the shade. It's amazing how much damage sun can do to the more delicate equipment—especially the mask. When the sun odometer hits 100,000 miles, you can kiss those soft parts good-bye.

Safety Inspections

Keep an eye on vulnerable parts after a few years (strap, snorkel-holder, buckles). Parts are usually easy to find on Maui, but not in the middle of a snorkeling trip unless you're on a well-equipped excursion.

If you use any equipment with purge valves, watch for sand on the delicate little flap valves. Also replace them when they deteriorate. Masks and snorkels are useless when the valves give way. Most snorkels now have a purge valve at the bottom, and some masks.

Clean Your Mask

A mask needs a thorough cleaning between trips. Unless your mask instructions advise otherwise, use a regular, non-gel toothpaste to clean the lens inside and out, polishing off accumulated goo. Wash the toothpaste off with warm water, using your finger to clean it well.

peacock grouper

Sign Language

Any serious snorkeler should bother to learn some basic signs starting with some of the standard scuba ones such as OK—meaning "Are you OK?", which should be answered with another OK; *palm up* for "stop", *wobbling hand* for "problem", and *thumb down*, meaning "heading down" (in this case referring to surface diving). This is an essential safety issue making it possible to communicate even if slightly separated or underwater. See a few of the signs below.

It's also a nuisance to take the snorkel out of your mouth every time you want to say "Did you see that moray!?!" Worse yet is trying to understand your buddy who frantically gestures and mumbles through the snorkel while you play charades. With a frequent snorkeling companion it's fun to develop signs for the creatures you might see. Eel can be indicated by three fingers looking like an E or by a wavy line drawn in the water. Then all you have to do is point and there it is!

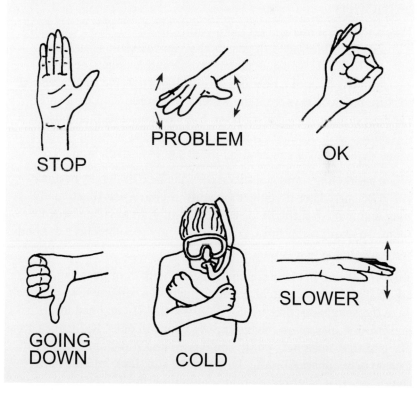

STOP

PROBLEM

OK

GOING DOWN

COLD

SLOWER

Hazards

Life just isn't safe. Snorkeling has a few hazards that you should know and avoid if possible. You already know the dangers of car and air travel, yet you mustered your courage and decided that a trip to Hawai'i was worth the risks. You took reasonable precautions like buckling your seat belt. Well, if you're sensible about it, you're safer in the water than while driving to get to the water.

Some people are hesitant to snorkel because they imagine meeting a scary creature in the water. But wouldn't you rather be able to see what's down there when you're swimming? We much prefer to see whatever we might step on or run into. The realities are seldom scary, and often beautiful instead. Don't let exaggerated risks keep you from enjoying life to the fullest.

We don't think it makes sense to overemphasize certain lurid but unlikely dangers (such as sharks) and pay no attention to the more likely hazard of sunburn which causes more aggravation to tourists.

Sunburn

This is the worst medical problem you're likely to face—especially if you weren't blessed with genetically sun-resistant skin. Lycra suits are better for you and the environment than sunscreen. The top (or open) deck of a boat is a serious hazard to the easily-burned because bounced rays from the water will double your exposure. The best protection is covering up. Evidence mounts that sunscreen still allows skin damage even though it stops the burning. Thanks to ozone depletion, we can now get more sun in a given hour.

When snorkeling, omit sunscreen on your face or hands, because you'll be sorry later if you get the stuff in your eyes. It can really sting and make it difficult to see well enough to navigate back to shore. To avoid using sunscreen, we strongly recommend lycra body suits. Or simply wear some old clothing.

Take an old sun hat to leave on the beach with your gear bag, especially if you have to hike midday across a reflective white beach. Take old sunglasses that are not theft-worthy. If you must leave prescription glasses on the beach, use your old ones. Kailua is a great place to find amazingly cheap sunglasses and flip-flops, such as at Costco or Walmart. For long hours in the sun, look into the better sunglasses that filter more of the damaging rays.

Understanding Waves

Waves are travelling ripples in the water, mostly generated by wind blowing over large expanses of water. Having considerable energy, the waves keep going until something stops them. They may travel many thousands of miles before dissipating that energy. Here is the wellspring of the breaking surf. That beautiful surf can also be the biggest danger facing snorkelers.

Take time to sit on a high point and watch the waves approaching the coast, and you will see patterns emerge. Usually there is an underlying groundswell from one direction, waves that may have originated in distant storms. This is the main source of the rhythmical breaking waves, rising and falling in size in noticeable patterns. Sometimes there will be a smaller secondary groundswell from another direction. Often, there will be a series of small waves, followed by one or more larger waves, and the cycle repeats. Pay attention to the patterns and it will be less likely that you'll get caught by surprise.

Local winds add extra energy in their own directions. In Hawai'i, snorkeling is usually easiest in the mornings, before the daily winds create chop and larger waves. Most excursions head out early to make sure they have smooth sailing and calm snorkeling. Sometimes afternoon excursions are offered at reduced prices to compensate for expected rougher conditions.

Occasionally a set of larger waves or a single large rogue wave comes in with little or no warning. A spot that was protected by an offshore reef suddenly has breaking waves. This change can happen while you're out, and make coming back difficult.

Our single worst moment in many years of snorkeling and diving was at Po'ipū Beach Park in Kaua'i after Hurricane 'Iniki had scattered boulders under the water. We had no problem snorkeling around the boulders in a light swell, protected by the reef further out. Suddenly much larger waves crossed the reef and began breaking over us, sweeping everyone back and forth among and against the boulders. Ouch!

Since then we have been extra careful to avoid potentially hazardous situations. We always take time to study the waves before entering and ponder what would happen if they suddenly grew much larger, and what our strategy would be. Sometimes we just head for a calmer beach.

Rip Currents

Hawai'i does not have large barrier reefs to intercept incoming waves. Many of Maui's beaches are exposed to the occasional powerful ocean swell—which is especially common in the winter or during storms.

Waves breaking against a shore push volumes of water up close to the shore. As this piles up, it has to flow back to the ocean, and often flows sideways along the shore until it reaches a convenient, often deeper-bottomed exit point. There, a fast, narrow river of water flows out at high speed. Rip currents, which can carry swimmers out quickly, are of limited duration by their very nature and usually stop no more than 100 yards out.

Sometimes it's possible to swim sideways, but often it's better to simply ride it out. Don't panic. Although the current might be very strong, it won't take you far or drown you, unless you exhaust

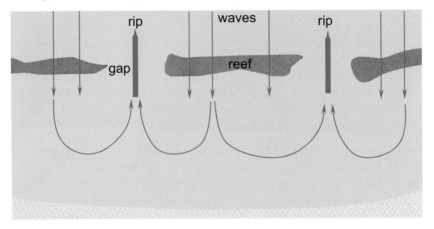

yourself by swimming against it. It's very easy to float in salt water until help arrives—assuming you're at a beach where someone can see you. Don't try to swim in through waves where there's any chance of being mashed on lava rocks or coral. Don't swim against the current to the point of exhaustion. When in doubt, float and conserve your energy, while you plan the safest way out.

Even at the most protected beaches all the water coming in must get out, so when swells are up, there's a current somewhere. Big waves beyond the breakwater may seem harmless, but the more water comes in, the more must get out. This is a good reason to ALWAYS wear fins even when the inner reef is calm.

Rip currents should not be confused with offshore currents, such as the infamous Tahiti Express. There are some major flows of water offshore that can be faster than you can swim even with fins. Do be alert and careful if you swim out beyond rocky points. Slowly test the direction you are moving when not swimming. Start your snorkel by swimming the more difficult direction, then you can coast back. Or travel swiftly with the current and send us a postcard from Tahiti.

Hypothermia

Open ocean water is always cooler than your body, and it cools you off more rapidly than the air. With normal exertion, your body still cools bit by bit. After awhile (perhaps 30-45 minutes) most of us start feeling chilly. Later, shivering begins. When your temperature drops even further, hypothermia sets in. When your body temperature has dropped enough, your abilities to move and even think become surprisingly impaired. It can sneak up on you.

We used to think hypothermia was just an interesting concept, until it happened to us after a long snorkel in some unusually cold water. We were shivering, but having a great time, and snorkeled on and on. Fortunately, we noticed the decrease in our co-ordination and headed in while we still could. You'd have laughed to see us stumbling clumsily out of the waves. We headed straight for the nearest jacuzzi (not recommended for full-blown hypothermia!). As we warmed up, our limbs tingled like fizzy water was going through our veins.

One of the first symptoms of hypothermia is poor judgement. Buddies can watch out for each other better than you can watch out for yourself alone—one example of the benefits of having a partner. Check up on each other often in cold water.

As soon as you are aware that you're cold, it's time to plan your way back. When shivering starts, you should head for shore immediately. Be particularly careful in situations requiring good judgement and skill to be safe, especially when diving, snorkeling at a remote beach, night snorkeling, dealing with waves, or when anticipating a difficult exit from the water.

In Hawai'i, it's usually easy to warm up rapidly since the air temperature is fairly warm at sea level. Even without hypothermia, it's good to warm up between snorkels. If you came by car, it will probably be nicely solar-heated by the time you return. We take gallon milk jugs of warm water to rinse off with at no-shower spots.

Sea Urchins

Probably the most common critter injury is stepping on a spiny sea urchin and walking away with lots of spines under your skin. The purple-black spiny sea urchins with long spines tend to appear in groups and favor shallow water, so watch carefully if you see even one — it probably has friends. Full-foot flippers or booties help a lot, but don't guarantee protection. Watch where you put your hands — especially in shallow water.

Many folks recommend seeing a doctor for urchin spine slivers. Others prefer to just let the spines fester and pop out weeks later. Remove as much spine as you can. Vinegar (or other acidic liquid) will make it feel better. Soaking in Epsom salts helps and the small spines will dissolve in a few weeks, but definitely see a doctor at any sign of infection. Don't wait for blood poisoning to set in!

banded sea urchin

Barracudas

The great barracuda can grow to two meters, has sharp teeth and strong jaws, and swims like a torpedo. For years Judy had removed earrings before swimming after hearing rumors that they attract barracuda, but we've uncovered absolutely no confirming reports of severed earlobes attributable to jewelry. But they can bite!

Barracudas are capable of seriously injuring a swimmer so should be taken seriously. Those teeth are just as sharp as they look. Barracudas appear to have attitude, and apparently sometimes do. Our own preference is to respect their territory and allow them some space. Other varieties of barracuda such as the smaller Heller's barracuda appear more innocuous. Appearances can deceive, however.

great barracuda

Once a four-foot great barracuda swam directly beneath us in the Caribbean and appeared annoyed that we were invading his home territory (or so we thought from the fierce look on his face). A usually calm and steady German surgeon headed up the nearest rocks as if she could fly. The rest of us snorkeled by him repeatedly with no problem, but didn't appreciate the look he gave us. We later came to realize that they always look grumpy, but seldom literally bite, like some folks you may know. Perhaps the bigger danger comes from eating the delicious barracuda meat, sometimes containing ciguatera, which is a potent neurotoxin.

Sea Jellies

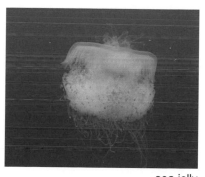
sea jelly

The Portuguese man-of-war floats on top, looking like a sail fin one to four inches in size, with long stinging filaments that are quite painful. Stay out of the water if you see one. Even avoid dead ones on the sand! They're very pretty in lovely shades of purple, but can cause severe pain.

Vinegar or unseasoned meat tenderizer helps ease the sting and helps stop the release of venom from the stinging cells if tentacles are clinging to you. Use wet sand as a last resort. If you feel ill, see a doctor right away. If sea jellies are present, locals will know which ones are harmful. Sea jellies have not been a problem for us in Hawai'i. In all our years in the water, we've only been stung by a Portuguese man-of-war once, not in Hawai'i, and it wasn't serious.

A reader recently reported getting little nips that were annoying. These could have been bits of hydroids floating around, or possibly small stinging sea jellies. Wearing a wetsuit or lycra would have taken care of that. Generally, these little nips have no long lasting effects, so it's best to not panic. Do avoid rubbing bare skin against mooring ropes, which often are covered with hydroids.

Rays

Sting rays prefer to avoid you, but hang out on the bottom where they're easy to step on. They prefer resting in calm water that is slightly warmer than the surrounding area—just the areas favored by people for swimming. Step on them and they may sting you, so the injury is usually to the foot or ankle. They can inflict a serious or painful sting to people—especially children. It's best to get immediate first aid and follow up with medical assistance.

In this case snorkelers have an advantage over swimmers because snorkelers can see sting rays and easily avoid them. In Maui we once saw them swim between children's legs in shallow water at Kapalua

cleaner wrasse on spotted eagle ray

Bay and were amazed to see how adept the rays were at avoiding people. They really try to steer clear.

Manta rays don't sting, but they're much larger. They are often six to eight feet across, weighing several hundred pounds. They maneuver beautifully, so they don't pose any danger. With a little luck and some planning, you may see one of these beautiful creatures.

Poisonous Fish

Lionfish (also called turkeyfish) and scorpionfish have spines which are very poisonous. Don't step on or touch them! Their poison can cause serious pain and infection or allergic reaction, so definitely see a doctor if you have a close, personal encounter with one. Fins or booties can help protect your tender feet.

Mel Malinowski

lionfish

Scorpionfish can blend in so well along the bottom in shallow water that they're easy to miss. Turkeyfish, though, are colorful and easy to spot. Since these fish are not abundant in Hawai'i, they are treasured sightings for snorkelers. You are not likely to see one while shallow-water snorkeling.

Eels

Eels are rarely aggressive and often tamed by divers. Most do possess a formidable array of teeth, which should be avoided. An eel bite can definitely cause serious bleeding requiring prompt medical attention. Another reason not to snorkel alone!

whitemouth moray eel

33

Eels are fascinating and easy to find in Hawai'i. Count on eels to make every effort to avoid you, so there's no need to panic at the sight of one—even if it's swimming freely. Eels aren't interested in humans as food, but they do want to protect themselves and can usually do so with ease by slipping away into the nearest hole. Do we need to warn you to keep your hands out of crevices in the coral?

Cone Shells

The snails inside these pretty black and brown-decorated shells can fire a poisonous dart. The venom can cause a serious reaction or even death—especially to allergic persons. If in doubt, head for a doctor. If you never pick up underwater shells, you should be OK.

Drowning

Not likely to happen to you, but we want to help you become so alert and prepared that you have a safe vacation. Accidental drowning is a very preventable tragedy.

We looked up the statistics for the past 30 years, and they are both comforting and cautionary. An average of 60 folks drown each year in all of Hawai'i. A much lower number than fatalities from auto wrecks, industrial accidents, or probably even accidents around the home, but not a group you want to join.

A couple things stand out about who are the victims. Three out of four victims are visitors. Not too surprising, since you assume locals are more aware of the hazards. But 80% are males, mostly 20 to 50 years old! You'd think this would be a low-risk group with adequate swimming skills.

What leads these fellows to get into a dangerous situation? Well, some guys just can't help overrating their athletic prowess, and perhaps underestimating the power of the ocean.

Some locations seem distinctly more hazardous. Beautiful Waipio Valley in the north can be calm as glass one day and great surfing the next. South swells can pick up in the summer making most of the beaches along the west fairly unpredictable.

It's easy to swim and snorkel in the island of Hawai'i safely. Improve your odds by checking which way the swells are rolling and picking protected beaches when the surf is pounding. Don't overestimate your stamina, or swim alone. Perhaps you might also follow our personal rule: always wear fins when swimming in the open ocean in Hawai'i—no matter how calm the water seems!

Sharks

Sharks are seldom a problem for snorkelers—people are not on their menu unless mistaken for legitimate prey or really obnoxious tourists. In Hawai'i deaths average less than one in two years with surfers the most common target because they look like seals. Sharks hunt in murky river runoff, but most snorkelers avoid these conditions anyway (our recommendation, too).

Statisticians tell us that you're more likely to be killed by a pig, dog or bee than a shark. We take great comfort in that, as I'm sure you do, too; though we've quit eating bacon just in case.

Mel Malinowski

blacktip reef shark

Some people will suggest you can pet, feed or even tease certain types of shark. We personally give sharks a bit of respect and leave them entirely in peace. Most sharks are well-fed on fish and not all that interested in ordinary tourists, but it's hard to tell by looking at a shark whether it has had a bad day.

Sharks mostly feed late in the late afternoon or at night, causing some people to prefer to enjoy the water more in the morning or midday. If you're in an area frequented by sharks, this might be good to keep in mind. We must admit that we snorkel at any hour, and occasionally night snorkel, and have had no problems.

In Hawai'i, with luck, you might possibly see sandbar, black-tip reef, white-tip reef or even hammerhead sharks—more often in deep water sites like Kealakekua Bay or near harbors. Of these, only hammerhead sharks should be avoided. Unless you're a surfer or swim way out from shore, your chances of ever seeing a tiger shark are very slim.

Snorkeling Sites

Where are those big beautiful fish?

Maui is justifiably famous as a swimming, sunning and snorkeling destination. Most of the great beaches are located on the more protected and relatively dry western side of the island.

For convenient snorkeling, the best areas to stay are West Maui (the Lahaina-Kā'anapali region), Kīhei (very central) or the Wailea/ Mākena area (in the southwest). Maui really isn't a large island, so most sites (apart from the Hāna area) are within an hour's drive if you stay along the west coast. Offshore sites are available by boat excursion from Lahaina and Mā'alaea Harbors.

West Maui offers numerous small, pretty bays. Some beaches have large hotels or condos. Other sites in the north have no facilities at all. Large waves in the winter make snorkeling difficult at some bays in the north, but bays shielded from swell can be surprisingly calm on the same day. Kīhei, located on flat land where the two mountains connect, is the most central place to stay and often has quite calm beaches. It has convenient access to the highways as well as lower-priced condos and long stretches of sand. While you can see some fish here, there is much better snorkeling and swimming not that far away. Kīhei doesn't have the charm or beauty of the north or south, but is a good base for exploring the island.

The Wailea/Mākena area, south of Kīhei offers huge hotels that have sprung up like wildflowers (or weeds, depending on whether you're staying there or having to walk through them to get to your favorite beach). Like West Maui, it offers small, undeveloped bays as well as large beaches surrounded by hotels with all amenities. These beaches aren't quite as protected as bays in the north, but they can be excellent when conditions are good. Drier than the north, the southwest has some strikingly beautiful beaches.

The entire west coast has plenty of hotels, condos, restaurants, shopping, excursions, hiking, golf and nightlife. The far north and the far south also are very close to some charming, nearly deserted spots. The tall mountains tend to catch most of the rain, so you will usually (but not always) have plenty of sun in these leeward areas. The long stretches of sand are wonderful for lounging, but in Maui, sand is a mixed blessing for snorkelers. Whenever swell rolls in, the

36

sand and sediment gets churned up, making the water a bit murky —especially after heavy rains, when muddy runoff flows to the sea. Don't expect 100 foot visibility, as some brochures imply, along the coast. There's still plenty to see, even with 30-60 foot visibility. Day trips to Molokini Island and Lāna'i can take you to clearer waters when you're in the mood.

Maui has small, calm bays with white sandy beaches that are perfect for beginners. Coral, colorful fish, eels, turtles, and more are in easy reach—exciting for beginners and experienced snorkelers alike. More advanced snorkelers can handle lava entries and snorkel out around points like Ulua-Mōkapu, Honolua, or Pu'u Ola'i.

There are countless excursions available to Molokini Island, and Lāna'i is just a short trip from Lahaina. The channel between these islands is shallow making for smooth trips most days. Consider taking either the ferry or an excursion to the friendly, uncrowded island of Lāna'i, where the snorkeling is excellent. If staying in the south, consider an excursion to the Kanaio Coast or Molokini.

In the site section ahead, you'll find snorkeling site reviews organized from Maui's far north, proceeding in counter-clockwise direction, with more details about our favorites as well as those with special appeal, such as good beginner beaches. You'll also find details about Molokini Island, as well as the island of Lāna'i, and a few tips about the (mostly boat-based) snorkeling on Moloka'i.

Many sites are surprisingly difficult to find, so bring these maps with you. People often drive up and down the highways with no idea which spots to try for snorkeling. Signs are scarce and small, so we've included maps and directions to help you find your spot.

Whatever your level of swimming or snorkeling ability, you can find a great spot to enjoy yourself along the west coast of Maui. When staying in the east, there are a few other sites farther afield (such as Hāna) that are worth a try. It's not possible to snorkel all the excellent sites in a week, so we hope that Snorkel Maui and Lāna'i will help you select a satisfying sample of the diverse snorkeling opportunities available on Maui, Lāna'i and Moloka'i.

When selecting a site, always consider direction of the swell. If the local paper says 8 foot north swell, stay away from bays that face north. When the swell comes from the south, you might find those northern bays calm as bath water. Conditions can change suddenly out here in the Pacific, so come to Maui prepared to be flexible.

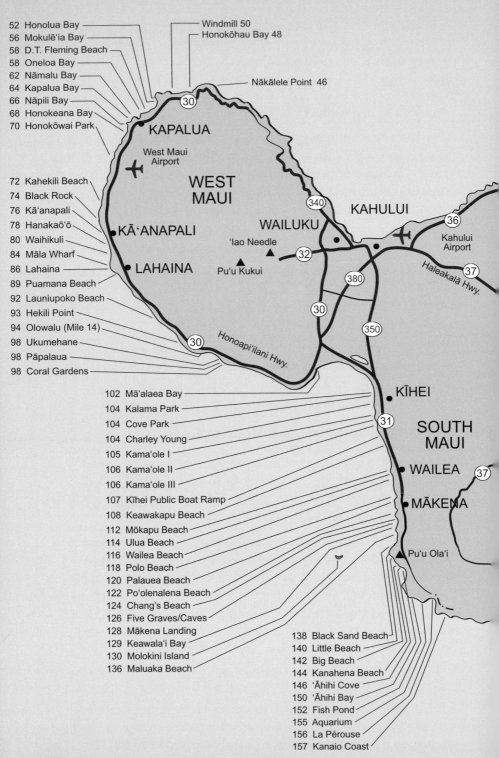

52 Honolua Bay
56 Mokulēʻia Bay
58 D.T. Fleming Beach
58 Oneloa Bay
62 Nāmalu Bay
64 Kapalua Bay
66 Nāpili Bay
68 Honokeana Bay
70 Honokōwai Park

Windmill 50
Honokōhau Bay 48

Nākālele Point 46

72 Kahekili Beach
74 Black Rock
76 Kāʻanapali
78 Hanakaōʻō
80 Waihikuli
84 Māla Wharf
86 Lahaina
89 Puamana Beach
92 Launiupoko Beach
93 Hekili Point
94 Olowalu (Mile 14)
98 Ukumehane
98 Pāpalaua
98 Coral Gardens

102 Māʻalaea Bay
104 Kalama Park
104 Cove Park
104 Charley Young
105 Kamaʻole I
106 Kamaʻole II
106 Kamaʻole III
107 Kīhei Public Boat Ramp
108 Keawakapu Beach
112 Mōkapu Beach
114 Ulua Beach
116 Wailea Beach
118 Polo Beach
120 Palauea Beach
122 Poʻolenalena Beach
124 Chang's Beach
126 Five Graves/Caves
128 Mākena Landing
129 Keawalaʻi Bay
130 Molokini Island
136 Maluaka Beach

138 Black Sand Beach
140 Little Beach
142 Big Beach
144 Kanahena Beach
146 ʻĀhihi Cove
150 ʻĀhihi Bay
152 Fish Pond
155 Aquarium
156 La Pérouse
157 Kanaio Coast

KAPALUA

West Maui
Airport

WEST
MAUI

KAHULUI

WAILUKU

Kahului
Airport

KĀʻANAPALI

ʻIao Needle

LAHAINA

Puʻu Kukui

Haleakalā Hwy.

Honoapiʻilani Hwy.

KĪHEI

SOUTH
MAUI

WAILEA

MĀKENA

Puʻu Olaʻi

38

Snorkel Site Index Map

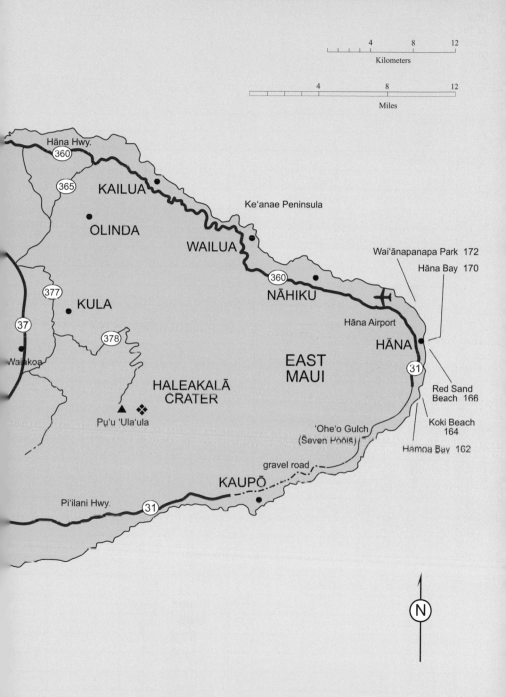

Kilometers
4   8   12

Miles
4   8   12

Hāna Hwy.
(360)

(365)   KAILUA

Ke'anae Peninsula

OLINDA

WAILUA

Wai'ānapanapa Park 172

(360)

Hāna Bay 170

(377)

NĀHIKU

KULA

Hāna Airport

(37)

(378)

HĀNA

Waiakoa

EAST
MAUI

(31)

HALEAKALĀ
CRATER

Red Sand
Beach 166

Pu'u 'Ula'ula

'Ohe'o Gulch
(Seven Pools)

Koki Beach
164

Hamoa Bay 162

gravel road

KAUPŌ

Pi'ilani Hwy.   (31)

N

Sites at a Glance

	Snorkeling	Entry	Sandy beach	Restroom	Showers	Picnic area	Scenic	Shade
Nākālele Point	C	3+					•	
Honokōhau Bay	A	2-3	•			•	•	•
Windmill	C	2-3	•			•	•	•
Honolua Bay	A	1					•	•
Mokulēʻia (Slaughterhouse)	B	1-3	•				•	•
D. T. Fleming Beach	B	3	•	•	•	•	•	•
Oneloa (Ironwoods)	B	3					•	•
Nāmalu Bay	B	2					•	•
Kapalua Bay	A	1	•	•	•	•	•	•
Nāpili Bay	B	1	•	•	•	•	•	•
Honokeana Bay	A	1-2			•		•	•
Honokōwai Park	C	2	•	•	•	•	•	•
Kahekili (Old Airport)	B	1	•	•	•	•	•	•
Black Rock (Kekaʻa)	B	1	•		•		•	•
Kāʻanapali Beach	C	1	•		•		•	•
Hanakaōʻō (Cemetery)	A	1-2	•	•	•	•	•	•
Waihikuli Wayside Park	B	1-2	•	•	•	•	•	•
Māla Wharf	B	1	•	•	•	•	•	•
Lahaina	C	1	•				•	•
Puamana Beach	C	1	•	•	•	•	•	•
Launiupoko Wayside	C	1-2	•	•	•	•	•	•
Hekili Point	C	1	•				•	•
Olowalu (Mile 14)	A	1	•	•		•	•	•
Ukumehame Beach	A	1-2	•			•	•	•
Pāpalaua (Coral Gardens)	A	1-2	•	•		•	•	•
Kalama Beach	C	1-2	•	•	•	•	•	•
Cove Park	C	1-2	•			•	•	•
Charley Young Beach	C	1-2	•	•	•	•	•	•
Kamaʻole I	B	1-2	•	•	•	•	•	•
Kamaʻole II	B	1-2	•	•	•	•	•	•

A	Excellent	1	Easy
B	Good	2	Moderate
C	Fair	3	Difficult

Page	Map page	
46	47	dangerous, remote, difficult entry, wild & pretty
48	47	lovely green valley, snorkel only when no north swell
50	51	too shallow for good snorkel or swim, nice picnic spot
52	53	fascinating & extensive large bay, only when calm
56	57	stairs to lovely bay, good snorkel & swim when calm
58	59	popular wide sand beach, often has huge waves
58	59	empty sand beach, but often has huge waves
62	63	small, slippery entry, walk to nearby Kapalua Bay
64	63	easy, pretty, usually calm enough, snorkel throughout
66	63	extensive calm bay near condos, more fish than coral
68	63	very hidden, excellent, easy snorkel, not deep
70	61	inner area very shallow, outer for experts
72	73	excellent beginner site, not too shallow or too deep
74	75	easy, popular & small, can be quite good at point
76	77	long sandy beach, better for swimming & sunbathing
78	79	pretty coral in 10-15'-deep water, near shore
80	79	best snorkel halfway between Hanakaō'ō & Waihikuli
84	85	tiny beach, turtles, maybe baby sharks, facilities
86	83	several small, swimmable spots, not much coral or fish
89	83	better for picnics than snorkel or swim
92	91	protected kiddie pool area, surfing & picnics
93	95	3-5' deep protected area, serves as baby fish nursery
94	95	usually calm, best coral and fish far from shore
98	91	good coral, but requires a swim to best area
98	91	best snorkel back toward Ukumehame & out a bit
104	101	good for kids, but not much coral, all amenities
104	101	tiny park, best for picnic, some fish, not much coral
104	101	tiny, pretty, great for picnic, little parking
105	101	lovely beach, better for boogie-boards and swimming
106	101	fine swimming, all facilities, nice family beach

Sites at a Glance

	Snorkeling	Entry	Sandy beach	Restroom	Showers	Picnic area	Scenic	Shade
Kama'ole III	B	1-2	•	•	•	•	•	•
Kīhei Boat Ramp	B	1-2	•	•	•	•	•	•
Keawakapu Beach	B	1	•	•	•	•	•	•
Mōkapu Beach	A	1	•	•	•	•	•	•
Ulua Beach	A	1	•	•	•	•	•	•
Wailea Beach	A	1	•	•	•	•	•	•
Polo Beach	B	2	•	•	•	•	•	•
Palauea Beach	A	1	•	•		•	•	•
Po'olenalena Beach	A	1	•	•		•	•	•
Chang's Beach (Mākena Surf)	A	1	•			•	•	
Five Graves/Caves	A	3					•	•
Mākena Landing	A	1	•	•	•	•	•	•
Keawala'i (Church Bay)	B	1-2	•	•	•		•	•
Molokini Island	A	1					•	
Maluaka Beach	A	1	•	•	•	•	•	•
Onuoli (Black Sand)	A	1-2	•			•	•	•
Pu'u Ola'i (Little Beach)	A	1-2	•					
Oneloa (Big Beach)	C	1-2	•	•		•	•	•
Kanehena Beach	C	2	•				•	•
'Āhihi Cove	A	1-2					•	
'Āhihi Bay	A	1-3	•	•		•	•	•
Fish Pond	A	1-2					•	
Aquarium	A	1-2					•	
La Pérouse Bay	A	2-3	•	•		•	•	•
Kanaio Coast	A	1					•	
Hāmoa Bay	C	1	•	•	•	•	•	•
Koki Beach	C	3	•	•		•	•	•
Red Sand Beach	A	1-3	•				•	•
Hāna Bay	A	1	•	•	•	•	•	•
Wai'ānapanapa Park	B	1-2	•	•		•	•	•

A	Excellent	1	Easy
B	Good	2	Moderate
C	Fair	3	Difficult

Page	Map page	
106	101	nice canopy trees, all facilities, excellent swimming
107	101	tiny sand entry, watch for boats, but room to explore
108	109	nice swim, easy snorkel, scattered coral & fish
112	111	popular, near large hotels, snorkel around point to Ulua
114	111	very popular, all amenities, reef extends far to sea
116	111	snorkel around point, turtles in deeper water
118	119	somewhat shallow & rocky, high tide best
120	119	long beach park, snorkel either end, uncrowded
122	119	north end best around small point, uncrowded
124	125	small, well-hidden, delightful spot for swim or snorkel
126	127	excellent when clear & calm, enter from lava rocks
128	127	tiny beach, long swim, but excellent snorkeling
129	127	tiny, hidden, uncrowded, usually easy access
130	131	boat access only, very clear water, excellent when calm
136	137	gorgeous, easy when calm, mornings best
138	137	whole bay fairly shallow, snorkel better than swim
140	135	short hike to nude beach, excellent snorkel when calm
142	135	great swimming, surfing & picnic area, popular, waves
144	135	hidden, tiny, lovely, usually too shallow to swim
146	147	small, but fun, shallow aquarium, milky water at times
150	147	excellent when calm, extensive area to explore
152	153	parking removed, long hike over very rough lava
155	153	hike in over lava or long swim, fragile reserve area
156	153	great only if calm & clear, requires fairly long swim
157	153	boat access only when calm, gorgeous black lava cliffs
162	163	beautiful beach, some snorkeling, better swimming
164	163	gorgeous spot to picnic, but usually has large waves
166	167	tricky hike, but excellent & unusual snorkeling
170	171	terrific and easy snorkeling near light when calm
172	173	often rough, but fun for advanced snorkelers, scenic

North Area

We start our tour around along the coast of Maui with the far northern area and continue in a counterclockwise direction.

The north is ruggedly beautiful and less crowded than the west or south. The water is very rough when there's big swell arriving from the north, which is most common in the winter. Summer can bring calm conditions here, while the south is getting big swell. Keep track of the weather and surf reports, then take a long hard look at any northern site before entering the water. Many are best left to experienced snorkelers in any weather.

Some of these sites, like Windmill, are very exposed and catch the full force of prevailing winds from the northeast. Honolua Bay is often calm (except for the more exposed far right).

Swells come from distant storms as well as prevailing winds and the lay of the land. A gradual sloping bay like Honolua at just the right angle can be fantastic and easy on some days, while neighboring Slaughterhouse is a bit too rough to enjoy.

Development is increasing in this area and will undoubtedly affect how pristine the reef remains. Brown algae and silt is covering some of the coral that was untouched just ten years ago. Fortunately the fish population is still outstanding in these picturesque bays.

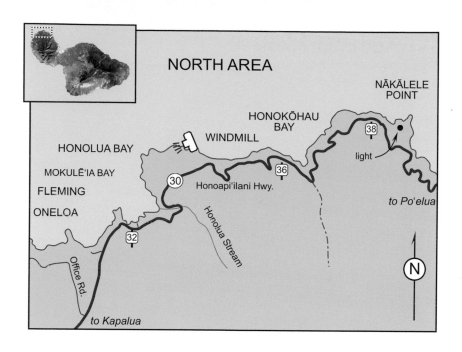

Map Symbols

Peak	▲	Location of picture	≋⌐
Place of interest	❖		
Highway	▬▬▬	Hotel or condominium	H
Paved road	▬▬▬	Parking area	P
Minor paved road	▬▬	Restroom	WC
Dirt road	–·–·–·	Lava	🪨
Foot path	- - - - -		
Road number	(50)	Sand	▦
Highway mileage marker	(11)	City	●
		Shower	⤷

Nākālele Point

Out of Maui's far northern shore, the winter waves have carved a rugged, but spectacular landscape of steep cliffs, arches, tiny coves, tidepools and blowholes. When the weather report predicts north swell, don't even think of swimming here, but on completely calm days, advanced snorkelers could consider this rocky coast. Pelagic fish are common due to exposure to the open ocean.

This north-facing site is the most difficult and dangerous entry we mention, so use extreme caution. There is always the possibility of a rogue wave smearing you like poi finger paint on the rocks. There are no lifeguards, and often no people in the vicinity.

Nākālele is worth the drive for its beauty alone, so consider enjoying the dramatic view rather than risking such a difficult entry. A spectacular view down to the rugged cliffs can be found by walking down the visible path straight toward the water.

The light station also provides an excellent view, but requires nearly a one-mile hike approaching from the right of the light. Late in the afternoon you can often see lots of turtles grazing along the edge of the rocks directly beneath the light. A large blow hole is often active around the corner to the right of the light. No facilities or crowds.

46

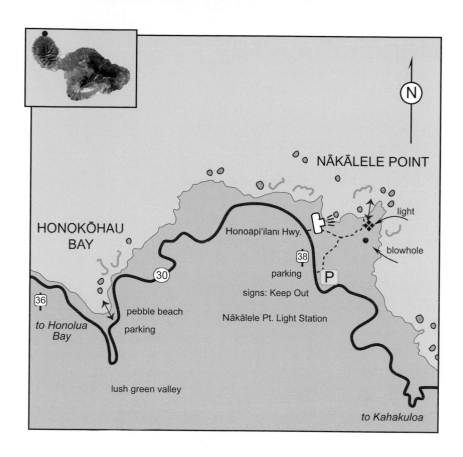

HONOKŌHAU BAY

NĀKĀLELE POINT

light

blowhole

Honoapi'ilani Hwy.

38

parking

P

signs: Keep Out

Nākālele Pt. Light Station

30

36

to Honolua Bay

pebble beach parking

lush green valley

to Kahakuloa

N

GETTING THERE

Take Highway 30 north past Lahaina and on past Honokōhau Bay (see area map, page 45). The highway is good, but narrow and winding north of Kapalua. The speed limits change frequently, so pay attention if you don't want to get a speeding ticket.

Look for mile marker 38, where you can park on the makai (ocean) side of the highway. Park in the dirt area along the highway and walk along the dirt path toward the light station, which can be seen from the highway. Walk toward the ironwood trees on the old 4WD road to your right in order to cross the gully and approach the light from the east.

To the right of the light station, you may get to see a dramatic blow hole spouting high in the air. When you arrive at the light (after about a half mile), you can look down on the area to snorkel. You'll see that this site involves a short, but fairly difficult climb and a risky entry. Once again—advanced snorkelers only.

Honokōhau Bay

Where this deep, lush valley, sculpted by eons of water runoff from the West Maui Mountains, reaches the ocean can be a beautiful spot to picnic, swim and snorkel. Large north swell in the winter makes it better suited to surfing at that time. Facing directly north, deep and narrow, Honokōhau is completely exposed to north swell when it arrives each year. Summer can find this bay flat, so watch the local wave report in the paper or online.

The valley is dramatic and tropical, a small oasis with a handful of houses near the bay. Plenty of parking is available right along the beach—a beach composed of pebbles rather than sand.

Snorkeling is best along the right side of the bay beyond any breaking waves. Enter carefully to avoid surf as well as small rocks on the bottom. Coral here tends to be quite small due to the rough conditions in winter, but you'll find plenty of interesting fish. Poke around the coral-encrusted large boulders. We have seen turtles, a snowflake eel, Christmas wrasses, and a variety of butterflyfish, wrasses and tangs.

Doctor My Eyes

If you are swimming along snorkeling peacefully and your vision suddenly loses focus, don't be too quick to panic and call for a doctor. While you may have had a stroke or the water may be oily, there is a much more likely cause: You've just entered into an outdoor demonstration of the refractive qualities of mixtures of clear liquids of different densities. Is that perfectly clear?

Near the edge of some protected bays, clear spring water oozes smoothly out into the saltwater. As it is lighter than the mineral-laden saltwater, it tends to float in a layer near the surface for a time. When you swim into it, you'll often notice a sudden drop in the water temperature. The fresh spring water can be downright chilly.

Now, clear spring water is easy to see through, as is clear saltwater. If you mix them thoroughly, you have dilute saltwater, still clear. But when the two float side by side, the light going through them is bent and re-bent as it passes between them, and this blurs your vision. It's much like the blurring produced when hot, lighter air rises off black pavement, and produces wavy vision and mirage.

These lenses of clear water drift about, and often disappear as quickly as they appeared. Swimming away from the source of the spring water usually solves the problem. You can also surface dive down a couple of feet to see the effect disappear. Are you clear at last?

When calm, this is a pretty spot for a swim, although the pebble beach isn't very comfortable on the feet. Once in the water, there's a mostly sandy bottom in the center of the bay.

GETTING THERE   Driving north on Highway 30, pass on by Lahaina. Watch for Honolua Bay and continue for another four miles past the Honolua entrance (see site map, page 47). Watch for highway marker 36 as the highway drops down towards Honokōhau Valley. You'll easily see the beach and ample parking area where people often camp. Portapotties and shade are available.

Windmill

Snorkeling is possible at Windmill (named for the steady winds), but it's really too shallow to enjoy—mostly one to four feet deep. This is a very popular camping and picnic spot for locals, who like to fish and spear octopus in the shallow, reef-protected area. If you want to snorkel, come at high tide for better clearance over the reef. This is definitely not a swimming beach.

The sign at the highway says "keep out". However locals have been using it as a park for many years, and that seems to be accepted. The road down to the beach is well-graded gravel and only about one tenth of a mile. Down near the water you'll find a long grove of ironwood trees, a beautiful view in both directions and a wide mixed pebble and sand beach protected by an outer reef. No facilities are available here. Plenty of parking and shade. Bring a picnic lunch and cool off in the stiff breeze.

GETTING THERE
Heading north on Highway 30 (see area map, page 45) past Kapalua, continue until you see mile marker 34. The road down to Windmill is six tenths of a mile beyond this marker. Turn left toward the ocean (makai) on this inconspicuous side road. It leads down to Windmill one-tenth of a mile. Or park along the highway where space permits and walk down the dirt road.

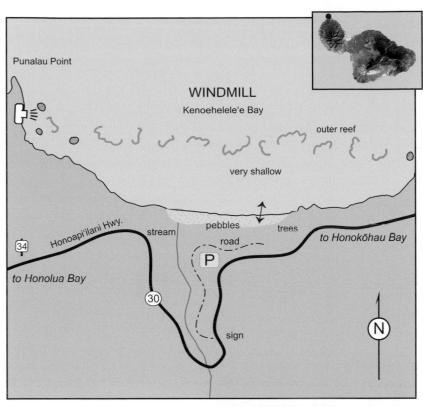

Punalau Point

WINDMILL

Kenoehelele'e Bay

outer reef

very shallow

Honoapi'ilani Hwy.

34

stream

pebbles

road

trees

P

to Honokōhau Bay

to Honolua Bay

30

sign

N

juvenile yellowtail coris

adult yellowtail coris

51

Honolua Bay

Part of Honolua-Mokulē'ia Bay Marine Life Conservation District, Honolua Bay is the larger bay just to the northeast. It has a famous surfing break off the northeastern point in the winter. The rest of the time, Honolua is usually quite well-protected and often flat and calm. Conditions here can change rapidly, so check the weather and surf report. It's common to have great surfing out to the right near the point at the same time as excellent snorkeling within the bay. You can catch a good view of conditions from the overlook.

When calm, Honolua Bay can be like a lake with some of the best snorkeling in all of Hawai'i. We typically see large parrotfish, turtles, big schools of barred goatfish, a variety of morays, big chubs and most of the usual Hawai'ian reef fish. Along the far right edge, we've also seen more than a thousand Hawai'ian flagtails—a school we couldn't even see through.

Honolua Bay turns brown after heavy rains when muddy creek water flows into the bay. From the highway overlooks on either side, it's easy to check for muddy water or large swells. On good days, you're likely to see lots of happy snorkelers exploring the bay. Come early because we've seen as many as five large snorkel boats in the bay—

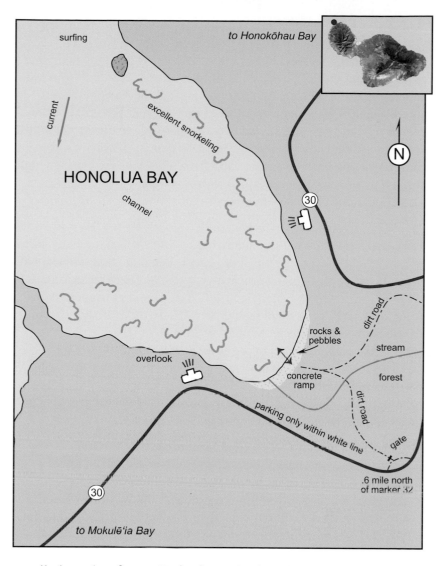

surfing

to Honokōhau Bay

current

excellent snorkeling

HONOLUA BAY

channel

N

30

rocks & pebbles

dirt road

stream

overlook

forest

concrete ramp

dirt road

parking only within white line

gate

.6 mile north of marker 32

30

to Mokulē'ia Bay

usually later than 9 a.m. Early risers also have less trouble finding convenient parking.

When calm, Honolua Bay is delightful and has something for everyone, beginner to advanced. You may enter anywhere along the rocky shore, but the easiest spot is in the center, where the dirt road ends. There are remnants of a small old concrete boat ramp at the water's edge. It's sometimes VERY slippery, so you should sit and work your way in slowly. We've often seen people underestimate how slippery concrete or rocks can be at the water's edge, then fall hard. Better to be cautious and stay low.

53

Snorkeling is best on the right side heading towards the point. The center has many fingers of coral with deep water between. We've seen many large fish and turtles there. The left is good too and often calmer, so snorkel all over the bay if time allows and conditions are favorable. If it's calm enough, snorkel around the point at the left into Mokulē'ia Bay, stopping short of the surf line. Be sure to check out all the little coves along the way. It's possible to have a delightful one-way snorkel into Mokulē'ia Bay now that a stairway has been built to get you back up to the road. These two bays are close enough for you to walk back on the highway to your car. It's even easier if you bring along flip-flops, booties or reef shoes in a net bag to tow along with you.

In Honolua Bay you will see many large, colorful fish, in many cases unusually big specimens: big chubs greet you, large tangs, bluespine unicorn surgeonfish, parrotfish, butterflyfish of many kinds, ornate wrasses, pearl wrasses, scrawled filefish, rectangular triggerfish, lei triggerfish, eels, turtles and much more. There often are big schools of fish such as blue-stripe snapper or Hawai'ian flagtails near the sides of the bay. Stay alert because we've seen octopuses, four-foot barracuda, and white-mouthed morays only ten feet from the concrete ramp entry. This is a beautiful spot for a rustic picnic under deep shade in a jungle setting, but it lacks a sandy beach, making it better for snorkeling than swimming. Don't miss this bay!

Go straight to Honolua when conditions are good. You'll definitely want to return. We've been here when south swell kicked up in the summer. Tourists in the south were despairing of finding a swimmable beach, but Honolua (completely unaffected by south swell) was calm as a bathtub. Few facilities here, but you'll find the closest at D. T. Fleming Beach (map, page 59) as you head for home.

multiband butterflyfish

GETTING THERE

Head north on Highway 30 past Kā'anapali and Kapalua. Continue past the fence and green railing at Mokulē'ia Bay for another half mile to where a dirt road dips down to Honolua Bay (see map, page 53). You can park along the road on the makai (ocean) side either before or after the dirt road with spaces easy to find early in the day. Be careful to park completely beyond the white line marking the edge of the traffic lanes. Walk around the car gate (always locked) and down along the dirt road. The short walk is easy and beautiful through this miniature rain forest. Rains can occasionally cause the creek to rise, so be prepared to wade through if necessary. Or drive further along the road to the second parking area noted on the map on page 57. You can always walk down the other dirt road there. It's twice the length of the main road, but a shady, pleasant walk.

The owner of most of the land surrounding Honolua Bay has proposed creating a public park here, complete with parking, restrooms and better access, in exchange for development concessions on other land they own mauka of the bay. We're guessing this process will go very slowly.

Mokulē'ia Bay

Often referred to by its nickname "Slaughterhouse", Mokulē'ia Bay is located just southwest of Honolua Bay, and is part of the same marine reserve. A wide, well-built concrete stairway makes access from the highway easy and opens up this pretty bay for picnics, swimming, boogie boarding, and snorkeling.

This site tends to have rougher surf than Honolua right next door, but has a nice sandy beach, shade trees, good swimming, picnicking and decent snorkeling just beyond the surf on the right. It has less coral and fish with more rubble than Honolua, but can be an excellent spot to see octopus or eel. Check our map on page 57 for the best spot to safely enter and snorkel to the right of the breakers. You will want to watch the swell for awhile to be certain it's safe to cross through low surf and arrive at the calm coves beyond. Beginners should stick with Honolua since swell at Mokulē'ia can change at any time making an exit more difficult at Mokulē'ia. Snorkelers can often safely snorkel around the point into Honolua Bay. When very calm, Mokulē'ia can provide a calm sandy beach for the easiest entry.

These two bays are not for any snorkeler when the surf gets heavy. Big swell rolls in often in the winter, and it can get rough any time of year if swell happens to arrive from the north. These bays then become fine surfing sites.

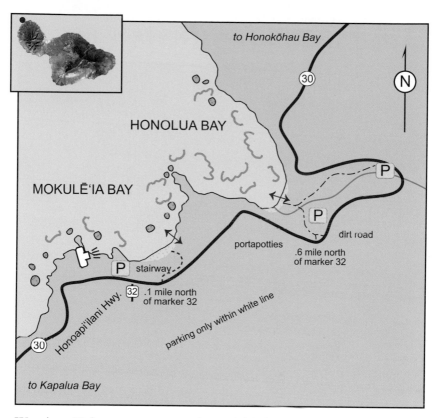

Map labels:
- to Honokōhau Bay
- (30)
- N
- HONOLUA BAY
- MOKULĒʻIA BAY
- P
- P
- P
- dirt road
- portapotties
- .6 mile north of marker 32
- stairway
- [32] .1 mile north of marker 32
- (30)
- Honoapiʻilani Hwy.
- parking only within white line
- to Kapalua Bay

Warning: Unless you are experienced, it's best to snorkel here in the mornings when quite calm, since waves can pick up unexpectedly and usually get bigger by noon. That said, sometimes late afternoon is wonderful and uncrowded, if that's when you can snorkel, go take a look and you may get lucky. No facilities, but nice for a picnic, swim or a little body surfing. Molulēʻia is a popular party spot in the evening and on weekends, sometimes complete with live music.

GETTING THERE
Go north on Highway 30 past Lahaina and Kapalua. Highway marker 31 is at D.T. Fleming Beach. Then watch for marker 32. Go one tenth of a mile past this marker. Watch for a painted green railing protecting you from the steep cliff. This marks the entrance to the sturdy Mokulēʻia Bay stairway. The beach is 88 steps down to the sand.

Parking is only allowed along the ocean (makai) side of the highway and limited to about thirty cars, so come early. You get an excellent view of Molulēʻia Bay from the top of the stairs, so check the swell from here. When swell is big, keep driving to Honolua Bay which is usually calmer—especially on the left side.

D.T. Fleming Park (Honokahua Bay)

A popular surfing and picnic spot with wide sand beach, lifeguards, showers, restrooms and picnic tables. There's plenty of reef near the breakers, but large surf pounds here most of the year, making it quite dangerous for snorkelers. This beach and Ironwoods next door face directly north. Ask the lifeguard before going in the water. When heading north, these are the last public facilities.

GETTING THERE   This beach is just northeast of the Kapalua area. Take Highway 30 to the first exit north of Kapalua and turn left toward the ocean. The park is located at the end of the road. You'll find a convenient shower to the right of the lifeguard and restrooms in front of the parking lot. A nice place to shower off if you've been snorkeling north of here. A pretty beach, nice for a picnic after a swim—and a lovely view of Moloka'i.

Oneloa Bay (Ironwoods)

This large bay (often called Ironwoods) lies just west of D.T. Fleming Beach. It has a similar wide sand beach facing due north with similar heavy surf most of the year, but has good snorkeling if you ever find it calm. It seems to catch every swell—we've seen it rough on days when Honolua Bay was flat as a pancake. Don't even

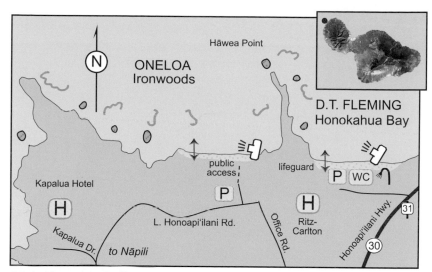

think about snorkeling here when waves roll in from the north—which is common in the winter. Water faucet on the left of the path. No other facilities. The road doesn't connect to D. T. Fleming Park right next door. You don't need to check out both of them since they catch identical waves.

GETTING THERE

This is the next beach NE of Namalu accessed by Office Road. Turn right toward the water at Ironwood Lane. You will immediately see a small public parking lot ("beach users only") before the gates. Take the marked concrete public access path (blue sign) down stairs to the sand.

West Area

Continuing in a counterclockwise direction, we come to the popular west side of West Maui, ranging from small Kapalua area bays, to the huge sand beach at Kāʻanapali, to tiny wayside parks along the side of the highway.

West Maui offers plenty of snorkeling and swimming sites. Hotels and condos at all price levels abound, but you won't find the most pristine beach conditions here. Nor will you have the beach or highway to yourselves. There is an abundance of sand and sun with some good snorkeling and plenty of excellent swimming. Some beaches are too shallow for the best swimming, but offer good snorkeling. Others (like Kāʻanapali) are huge and better for swimming. However, Black Rock (at the north end of Kāʻanapali) provides excellent snorkeling.

On the whole these sites are better for swimming, but Honokeana and Kahekili are better snorkeling destinations. Black Rock is small and has little parking, but is very popular with snorkelers. Some beaches, such as Puamana, are best left to the surfers. We will proceed with Namalu Bay, the northernmost of these western sites and continue counterclockwise to Waihikuli in the south. We mentioned only the beaches that are deep enough for water sports, not the ones with poor access over shallow coral.

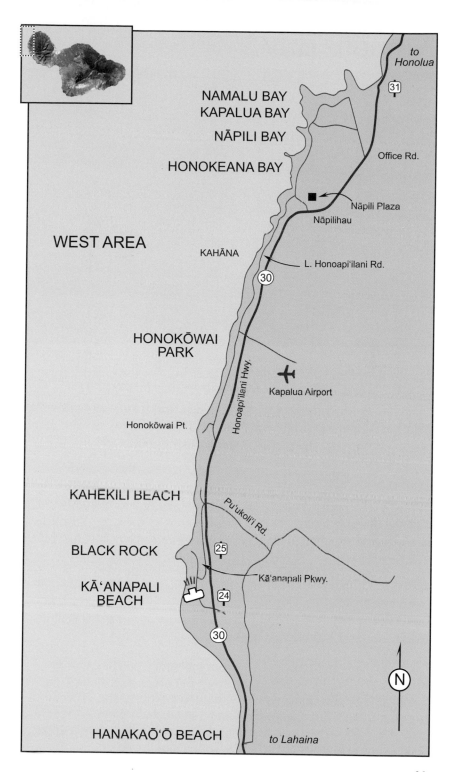

to
Honolua

31

NAMALU BAY
KAPALUA BAY
NĀPILI BAY
HONOKEANA BAY

Office Rd.

Nāpili Plaza
Nāpilihau

WEST AREA

KAHĀNA

L. Honoapi'ilani Rd.

30

HONOKŌWAI
PARK

Honoapi'ilani Hwy.

Kapalua Airport

Honokōwai Pt.

KAHEKILI BEACH

Pu'ukoli'i Rd.

BLACK ROCK

25

KĀ'ANAPALI
BEACH

Kā'anapali Pkwy.

24

30

N

HANAKAŌ'Ō BEACH

to Lahaina

61

Namalu Bay

Just north of Kapalua Bay and directly in front of the Residences at Kapalua, you'll find a small, pretty bay. The rocky entry can be very slippery, the water tends to be a bit choppy, and it has less to offer, so most snorkelers will prefer Kapalua Bay. When the bay is calm, it's possible to snorkel all the way to the northern point.

As you swim to the north through boulder terrain, the water deepens with drop-offs up to thirty feet. It's dramatic underwater rocky terrain, rather pretty. You'll find little coral, but a decent number of fish and possibly a turtle or two. We've seen yellow tangs, teardrop butterflyfish, Moorish idols, parrotfish, Christmas wrasses, lots of orangespine surgeonfish and even a few pearl wrasses.

When it's calm, good swimmers can snorkel around the point at the left into Kapalua Bay. Don't try this when swell is rolling in! Take time to float and look around you at the picturesque natural setting, with Lāna'i and Moloka'i in the background.

GETTING THERE
From the public parking area for Kapalua Bay (access #219), walk down the steps and through the tunnel to the right. Continue on the path to the north end of broad Kapalua Beach. From there it's about 100 yards through the resort grounds. Walk on out past the point, and down to the water's edge, taking care to avoid slipping on the algae near the water.

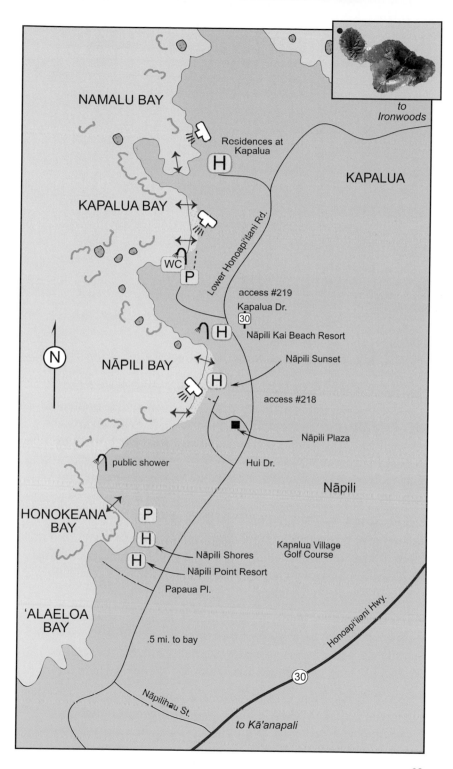

NAMALU BAY

to
Ironwoods

Residences at
Kapalua

H

KAPALUA

KAPALUA BAY

WC

P

Lower Honoapiʻilani Rd.

access #219
Kapalua Dr.

30

H

Nāpili Kai Beach Resort

Nāpili Sunset

N

NĀPILI BAY

H

access #218

H

Nāpili Plaza

public shower

Hui Dr.

Nāpili

HONOKEANA
BAY

P

H

Kapalua Village
Golf Course

H

Nāpili Shores

Nāpili Point Resort

Papaua Pl.

'ALAELOA
BAY

.5 mi. to bay

Honoapiʻilani Hwy.

Nāpilihau St.

30

to Kā'anapali

63

Kapalua Bay

This popular beach just south of the Kapalua Bay Resort has very good snorkeling, excellent swimming in the center and easy entry anywhere along its crescent of sand—making it an excellent choice for beginners. This area is a great location for snorkelers to stay since it provides relatively calm swimming and snorkeling as well as quick access (ten minutes by car) to excellent northern sites such as Honolua Bay.

The best snorkeling at Kapalua Bay is on the right as far as the point, although the whole bay is interesting: left, center and even close to shore. When the water is calm (more likely in the summer), you can get close to the edges. When there is more swell, avoid the shallow areas and watch out for currents.

We like to swim out along the left side, close to the rocks. While there is little coral here, you get up close views of interesting small fish such as belted wrasse, pearl wrasse and ambon toby. Follow the curve around, not getting into water too shallow (where the waves break).

When you get out to where a line could be drawn from left point to right point, swim across to the right. As you near the right side, you'll cross a rocky shelf in about twenty feet of water with sandy breaks on the far side. This is a good spot to see schools of goatfish, as well as eyestripe surgeonfish. Swim back along the right side. Close in, you can see big bluespine unicorn surgeonfish, orangespine surgeonfish, and goatfish of several types. We've even seen a great barracuda, as well as a zebra moray eel.

When the summer south swell surf kicks up along the west coast, try heading here because it's often as calm as Maui gets. Public parking is limited to about 25 cars and the lot fills early. There is no alternative parking available anywhere close now that parking isn't allowed along the road.

Kapalua Bay tends to stay calm and the crowds ease in the afternoon. Showers and restrooms are available on the beach side of the public parking lot. Once you find a parking space, the path to the beach is short—down a few steps, through a tunnel and there's the beach!

The bay is small, so you can swim around the whole area if you wish. We have seen eels, turtles, an octopus, as well as most of the many colorful fish that call Maui home. When seas are unusually calm, a strong swimmer can snorkel around the point to the left and end up at Nāpili Bay—only a short hike back to your car if you cut through the condo developments. If you decide to try this, the best place to exit is the sandy corner near the shower (see map, page 63).

GETTING THERE
Kapalua Bay has just one public access, #219 (see map, page 63). Look sharp, since it's easy to miss the tiny blue access sign. Parking fills up early, but often has plenty of space later in the late afternoon. Drive north on Highway 30, past Kā'anapali and take the next major Y to the left, which is Lower Honoapi'ilani Road.

Following the coast, just one tenth of a mile north of marker 30, you'll see the Nāpili Kai Beach Club on your left and a tiny blue beach access sign. Turn left here and park in the public lot at the end of the road on the right. You'll see the showers and restrooms toward the beach. To the right of the restrooms, follow the path down steps into a short tunnel. Entry to the bay is usually easy anywhere along the broad sandy beach. Swim along the reef on the left side of the bay.

Or take Highway 30 north and turn left on Nāpilihau Street. Then turn right on Lower Honoapi'ilani Road. Watch for mile marker 30 and you'll find the blue access sign just one-tenth of a mile to the north. Turn left here at the Nāpili Kai Beach Club. The little blue access signs sometimes disappear, making the beach access points difficult to find, so always check mileage carefully.

Nāpili Bay

Much larger than Kapalua Bay, this inviting bay to the south is a beautiful place to picnic, swim, sun or snorkel. Nāpili Bay is completely surrounded by condos, so there are often plenty of people here enjoying the sandy beach. If you want to snorkel, park anywhere because you can enter the water at either end or middle. Although Nāpili Bay has three public accesses, there is little parking available, so come very early in the morning or late in the afternoon.

Entry is easiest from the sand anywhere along the beach, but you can also enter from the rocks in several places from the path in front of the condos along the right point. If you enter from the right side of the beach, you'll have to swim over toward the center a bit to get around a very shallow rocky shelf just offshore at the right end. As you head out along the rocky right side, watch in the many cracks for hawkfish, eels and other critters. We've seen a zebra moray eel here, as well as pearl wrasse, boxfish, cigar wrasse, ambon tobies, cowries, cone shells, large turtles, rectangular triggerfish and big schools of bluespine unicornfish. There is very little coral. One unusual feature of this bay is that the slope is very gradual, so even far out in the bay, the water is only ten feet deep.

There is a rocky shelf in the middle of the bay, extending from side to side (mentioned above). You can swim across it in the middle of the bay, and also at the far left. Most of the right side of the bay is a broad sand flat with few fish. The left side of the bay has almost no coral, but there are many fish among the rocky formations interspersed with sandy patches.

A small simple shower is available along the public access path #218, but the nearest public restrooms are located at the Kapalua parking lot (access #219).

The near shore at Nāpili Bay slopes more steeply than nearby beaches in the winter. Studies have shown that if you build too close to the beach, then as natural erosion tries to move the beach further inland, it cannot—resulting in less and less beach! When the sand has been taken out by winter waves, the beach is narrow and the surf develops a good backwards tow. It can shoot you up on the sand and just as quickly slide you right back into the water—a great way to fill your bathing suit with sand. Kids will love it. Just watch little ones very carefully when there's any surf at all. When all the sand returns in the summer, Nāpili is a delightful family swimming beach.

GETTING THERE
Nāpili has two public beach access signs, but both are easy to miss, and neither offers much parking (see site map, page 63). Going north on Highway 30 past Kāʻanapali, turn left at the Nāpili exit (Nāpilihau St. at mile marker 29). Turn right when it hits Lower Honoapiʻilani Road, and continue to the north (right) past ʻAlaeloa.

When you see signs for the various Nāpili Bay condos, watch for little blue beach access signs. Access point #219 is the furthest north, so using it gets you closer to the snorkeling. Walk to the left instead of the right (Kapalua Bay is to the right). There is a small public shower tucked away at the corner of the beach along the walkway in front of the condos.

Access point #218 is hidden (see map, page 63) behind a small shopping center (Nāpili Plaza) on Lower Honoapiʻilani. Just continue driving through the shopping center toward the water past Snorkel Bob's (ignoring the warning sign) and there is access #218! You'll even find a small public shower along this short path to the water.

From Lower Honoapiʻilani (heading north) you can also take a left on little Hui Road to get to this access. Parking is another matter! Most people who use Nāpili Bay are staying in one of the many condos along the shore.

Honokeana Bay

This totally hidden little bay offers good snorkeling and typically calm water, but it's hard to find and offers no designated parking or marked public access. What you'll find is a pretty, shallow bay completely surrounded by condos perched on small hills overlooking the bay. Since there is a path from Nāpili Beach, this seems to be public access, although it isn't marked. Besides the path along the north point to Nāpili Beach, the only way to access Honokeana is through the adjoining condos.

When conditions are rough elsewhere, you might consider trying Honokeana if limited parking is available. We also see divers and snorkelers park in the far corners of the Nāpili Shores Resort. There is no beach to speak of, so entry is from lava on the north side of the bay in front of the resort. This whole bay is well-protected by an outer reef and is about the perfect depth for good snorkeling (three to ten feet). The coral isn't spectacular, but we have seen turtles, lots of rectangular triggerfish, teardrop and raccoon butterflyfish, unicornfish, snowflake moray, belted wrasses, and even some pretty pearl wrasses.

Honokeana Bay is excellent for beginners providing you walk carefully across the lava and don't slip when you enter and exit. Even easier, there's sometimes a tiny sandy area at the eastern end of the bay. Just follow the path toward the center of the bay.

You'll find just enough here to keep any snorkeler happy. Be sure to check it out—especially if conditions aren't too calm elsewhere. Honokeana Bay is usually well-sheltered from swells as well as from wind. It's just deep enough for good swimming if you don't mind the absence of a beach.

GETTING THERE
Heading north on Highway 30, turn left at the Nāpili exit (Nāpilihau Street). Then turn right when you get to Lower Honoapi'ilani Road (see site map, page 63). Pass Kapalua Place on your left and watch for Nāpili Point Resort. Park in the small off-street gravel areas and walk through the parking lot just north of the resort and before Da Store. About 2/3 of the way through the parking lot, go left at the sign to building A. You will immediately see a lovely bay. Enter from the lava rocks directly in front of you, assuming the bay is calm. It that looks difficult, turn left toward the center of the bay. The hidden shower can be found along the path toward the point at the north—follow a concrete path to the ocean edge between Nāpili Point and Nāpili Shores.

'Alaeloa Bay

This charming little beach, without much sand, looks like it could have some snorkeling with space to explore from a pebbled entry. Getting to the beach is the main problem, since the only land access is across private property. The surrounding development is gated and the houses are rented on a monthly basis, so it isn't easy to gain entrance. This development went in before public access was required and they seem quite determined to keep it private. Given the difficulty of access, we have decided to not snorkel or review it.

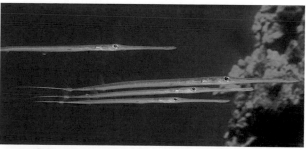

cornetfish

Honokōwai Park

The reef here is very shallow, making swimming difficult and a bit hazardous at times. At low tide, however, there are tide pools perfect for young children. Only the ocean side of the reef is deep enough for easy snorkeling, so go on a very calm day at high tide. To get beyond the shallow part, swim out at the far north of the park (to your right). This is not a good place for beginners. You'll find a shady, grassy park with picnic tables, facilities, and a store right across the street in case you forgot to bring a picnic.

GETTING THERE

This park is easy to spot along Lower Honoapiʻilani Road and has plenty of parking (see area map, page 61). Going north from Kāʻanapali on Highway 30, angle left on Lower Honoapiʻilani Road and watch for the first beach makai (ocean side). You'll find the park across the street from the Farmer's Market and Boss Frog's. On the ocean side you will see a square grassy area with shade trees, picnic tables, restrooms, kid's playground, and shower.

Snuba

Snuba was developed as a simpler alternative to scuba for shallow dives in resort conditions. Because Snuba divers are strictly limited in depth and conditions, and are always accompanied by a guide, the orientation takes just 15-30 minutes.

Two people share a small inflatable raft, which holds a scuba air tank. A twenty-foot hose leads from the tank to a light harness on each diver. A comfortable weight belt completes your outfit. Very light and tropical!

Once in the water, your guide teaches you to breathe through your regulator (which has a mouthpiece just like your snorkel) on the surface until you're completely comfortable. You're then free to swim around as you like, remembering to clear your ears as needed (limited by the hose to twenty feet deep, of course).

The raft will automatically follow you as you tour the reef. It's that easy! You have to be at least eight years old, and have normal good health. Kids do amazingly well, and senior citizens can also enjoy Snuba. There's even a new program called Snuba Doo for four to seven-year-old children. They wear a flotation vest, and breathe through a regulator as they float on the surface while their parents Snuba below.

We are certified scuba divers, yet we often enjoy Snuba more. Less gear equals more fun. Snuba is a lot like snorkeling, with the added freedom to get down close to fish and coral. We often surface dive to check out what fish is hiding under a coral head. Snuba is like surface diving without having to come up for air!

Snuba provides a fun and safe experience if you pay attention and do it as directed. Their safety record is superb.

Warning: do pay attention to the instructions because even at these shallow depths, you must know the proper way to surface. You must remember to never hold your breath as you ascend or you could force a bubble of air into your blood. Breathing out continually while surfacing is not intuitive, but is absolutely necessary when you're breathing compressed air. This is especially important to remember if you're used to surface diving where you always hold your breath. Dive safely!

Kahekili Beach Park (Old Airport)

This pleasant beach park is popular with locals and divers, but very easy to miss, well hidden by large new condo developments. With a gentle sandy beach, it's a perfect spot for beginners and usually quite calm. Often called Old Airport Beach, it's near the former site of the West Maui Airport.

We prefer to snorkel to the right from the northern boundary of the park. The reef here is easy to find, near shore and just about the perfect depth (three to ten feet).

The snorkeling area runs for about a mile north offering a chance to wander and enjoy. While not spectacular, the coral and fish are interesting if you take the time to watch carefully. Beginners who find Olowalu too shallow for comfort will like the extra clearance at Kahekili Beach Park.

We were trailed by hungry unicornfish looking for a handout—a sure sign that someone has been feeding them in this area (not a good idea!). We also saw groups of raccoon butterflyfish, several eels, an octopus, turtles and even a fantail triggerfish. The coral is pretty and healthy, but not large. Kahekili is open 6 a.m. until 1/2 hour after sunset. It has restrooms, a shower, shade trees, grass,

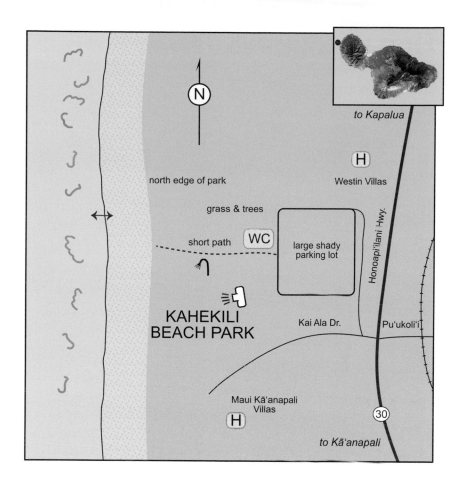

picnic tables, barbecue grills, ample parking lot and a lovely view of Lāna'i. More advanced snorkelers may want to snorkel a half mile to the north. When a slow current runs south, swim against it as far as comfortable, then catch a faster ride back to the park. You're always close to shore with an easy and sandy exit all along the way.

GETTING THERE

Go north on Highway 30 until the last exit for Kā'anapali (see area map, page 61). This intersection is called Kai Ala Drive on the ocean side (makai) and Pu'ukali'i Road towards the mountains (mauka). Turn left toward the ocean and angle right into the parking lot rather than left to the Maui Kā'anapali Villas. You'll find plenty of parking with most of it in the shade.

Kahekili is across the highway from a Sugar Train station, so you can snorkel to train sounds in the background as well as planes flying directly overhead as they approach the Kapalua Airport.

Black Rock (Keka'a Point)

The ever-popular point occupied by the Sheraton offers fairly good snorkeling, though it is only modestly endowed with coral and fish. This is a pretty enough spot to make it worth your while finding a parking spot—the major challenge. Shoreline access #213 (see map, page 75) is located between the Sheraton Maui and the Kā'anapali Beach Hotel. The access sign and path are easy to find, but parking is quite another matter. The Sheraton provides a small corner of its parking structure for the public. Check our map, then come early (certainly before 9 a.m.) to nab one of the twenty spaces. Otherwise you will have to wait for someone to leave, park illegally or pay to park at Whaler's Village. Some people manage to convince neighboring hotels to valet park their car for $5 or so. That certainly won't work on a weekend or holiday when everything fills.

From the sand, head to the north end of the beach and snorkel along the rocky cliff as far as it's calm. Often you can round the point, stopping to explore nooks and crannies along the way. Beginners should stay where the water is flat, but experienced snorkelers can easily swim all the way around the point when the water is calm.

While there isn't much coral here, the fish are varied and somewhat tame, so you do get a good look. We've enjoyed watching a bold

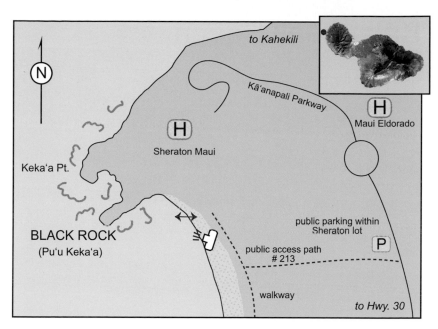

octopus near the point, saw a couple of spotted eagle rays cruising the point, as well as a variety of tangs, triggerfish, needlefish and cornetfish. Watch for pairs of several kinds of butterflyfish such as the teardrop and the oval. Watch closely. We saw an octopus on the rocks about five feet from the surface, but all the other snorkelers zipped on past without spotting it. By now, we have what locals call "the tako eye". Tako is the Japanese word for octopus.

There are no designated public facilities here, but the big hotels have showers at the edge of the sand

GETTING THERE

Heading north past Lahaina on Highway 30, take the main Kāʻanapali turnoff called Kāʻanapali Parkway (see map, page 77). Follow the Parkway to the right toward access #213 just south of the Westin Kāʻanapali Villas. On this divided road continue slowly until you see the sign for the public access path just before the parking garage. You'll have to continue a bit further on this divided road until you can make a U-turn. The public parking entrance is easy to miss. It's located in the southern corner of the Westin Kāʻanapali Villas garage, which is immediately north of the public access path.

When these spaces are filled, you might find a spot further south at any of several beach access parking areas (marked on our map). A walkway on the ocean side of the hotels will get you to Black Rock, but it can be a long hike. Whaler's Village has a pay parking lot.

75

Kāʻanapali Beach

Kāʻanapali Beach, except for Black Rock, is better for swimming and people watching than snorkeling. People are starting to call it DigMe Beach because it's THE place to see and be seen. If you're not staying at a local hotel, you'll need to find a parking space before you can start socializing.

GETTING THERE   There are four more public access paths besides the Westin Kāʻanapali Villas (all with limited parking) along the rest of Kāʻanapali. Heading north on Highway 30, take the main exit called Kāʻanapali Parkway, then turn left at the hotels.

The first public access going south is #212 just south of Whaler's Village (see site map, page 75). There are about fifty designated, but scattered spaces in this parking lot and the path is found just to the south of the parking lot.

The next public access is #211 between the Westin and the Kāʻanapali Aliʻi. It's easy to miss, doesn't have obvious parking, and provides a 200-yard path to the sand.

Access #210 has ten parking spaces and is located between the Kāʻanapali Aliʻi and the Marriott. The path is just south of parking.

Access #209 has about 25 spaces and is found between the Marriott and the Hyatt. Again, the path is just south of the public parking.

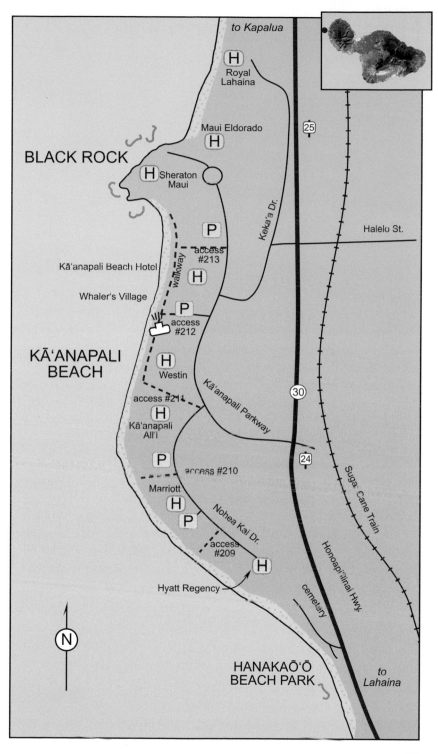

to Kapalua

H Royal Lahaina

Maui Eldorado H

BLACK ROCK

H Sheraton Maui

25

Keka'a Dr.

P

access #213

Kā'anapali Beach Hotel

walkway

H

Whaler's Village

P

access #212

KĀ'ANAPALI BEACH

H Westin

Halelo St.

access #211

H Kā'anapali Ali'i

Kā'anapali Parkway

30

P

access #210

24

Marriott H

P

Nohea Kai Dr.

access #209

H

Sugar Cane Train

Hyatt Regency

cemetery

Honoapi'ilani Hwy.

N

HANAKAŌ'Ō BEACH PARK

to Lahaina

Hanakaō‘ō Beach (Cemetery)

Located south of Kāʻanapali, stretching along Highway 30 starting at Hanakaō‘ō Cemetery in the north. Lots of parking, lifeguards, restrooms, shower, grass and shade trees. Park as far south as possible to enter from a sandy beach. While surfers wait for waves directly in front of the lifeguard station, the area south of the park offers good snorkeling and is usually calm and relatively clear.

We like to enter from the sand and snorkel south to the next park. This takes you through plenty of interesting coral and fish. When calm, it's an easy shallow snorkel—with comfortable depth (five to ten feet) close to shore. Don't worry if you pass a great barracuda looking mean and territorial. We also have seen some large bluespine unicornfish, big schools of goat fish, and healthy coral in shades of lavender, green, yellow, orange and pink. The snorkeling spots we like best are on either side of the culvert halfway between Hanakaō‘ō and Waihikuli parks.

In calm weather, this is a good site for beginners with easy entry from sand, good depth and not far from shore. You will definitely want to enter and exit from the sand rather than the lava.

There is now a popular jet ski "island" right in front of the park. While we would hope they would all stay well beyond swimmers, we're not sure you can count on it. Stay fairly close to the shore.

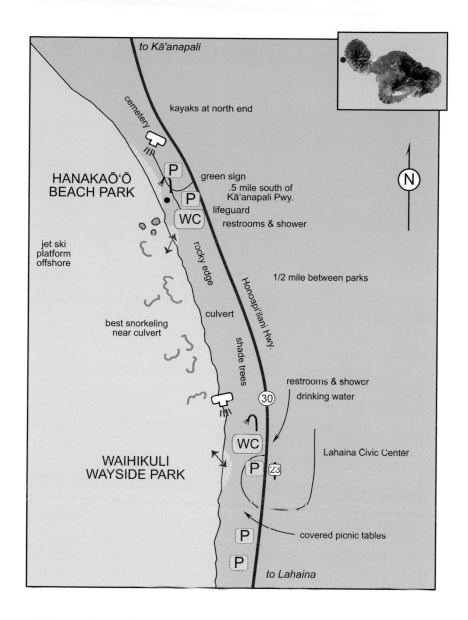

to Kāʻanapali

kayaks at north end

cemetery

**HANAKAŌʻŌ
BEACH PARK**

P

green sign
.5 mile south of
Kāʻanapali Pwy.

lifeguard

WC

restrooms & shower

jet ski
platform
offshore

rocky edge

1/2 mile between parks

Honoapiʻilani Hwy.

culvert

best snorkeling
near culvert

shade trees

restrooms & shower

(30) drinking water

WC

**WAIHIKULI
WAYSIDE PARK**

Lahaina Civic Center

P 23

P

covered picnic tables

P

to Lahaina

N

GETTING THERE

From Lahaina, go north on Highway 30 watching for mile marker 23 (near the post office and county buildings mauka). Continue north to the next beach park on your left.

From Kāʻanapali, head south on Highway 30. The park entrance is half a mile south of Kāʻanapali Parkway. Turn toward the water, then left to park in the southernmost parking lot for easy access to the beach. Snorkel to the left (south) and don't wander too far from shore (because of the jet skis).

79

Waihikuli Wayside Park

This narrow strip along the makai (ocean) side of Highway 30 offers parking, covered picnic tables, grass and shade at three separate sections in a row. Only the northern section offers restrooms and a good shower. Most of the coast is rocky here, so entry is from the tiny bits of sandy beach—best from the middle section. The small, scattered parking areas are easily visible from the highway. While you can snorkel here, conditions are sometimes a bit calmer further south or north. When little waves slap the shore, walk out on the sand carrying your fins to put on where it's calm.

Experienced snorkelers might want to enter the water here for a one-way snorkel to Hanakaōʻō Beach Park (the next beach to the north). Entry is easier at Hanakaōʻō, but the good snorkeling is about halfway in between (see site map, page 79). Waihikuli and Hanakaʻōʻō are about half a mile apart with decent snorkeling near shore in about five to ten feet of water. The best coral is on either side of the culvert.

GETTING THERE

Heading north on Highway 30 from Olowalu, watch for highway marker 23 just after the turnoff on your right for the Lahaina Civic Center (see site map, page 79). At marker 23, turn left toward the ocean to enter the park. Enter the water at the sandy beach and snorkel north for the best snorkeling. Our favorite spot here is about a quarter mile north and close to the shore. Don't stray way out to sea since that could put you in the path of those speeding jet skis. For a sandy entrance, choose the north or middle lot of the three parking lots (pictured above). For facilities, choose the one furthest to the north.

80

Snorkeling Grad School

We expect that some of you will progress to advanced snorkeling. Here are a few tips gleaned from our thousands of happy hours paddling around in the salty seas.

Now that you know many of the common fish of Hawai'i, take it up a notch or two by going places you might have neglected, such as shallow rocky areas, the surge zone, and deep dropoffs. You'll begin to see fish and critters that are not depicted on those plastic fish guides. If you have a curious nature, it's tons of fun.

We love to snorkel in the shallow areas at the fringes of many bays. At some sites, this may be 2 to 5-foot deep rubble, not very pretty at first glance. But if you are patient, and look closely, here is where you'll find the spectacular snowflake moray eel, octopus, Picasso triggerfish, cute tiny juvenile stages of reef fish such as the yellowtail coris (which looks a lot like Nemo) and sailfin tangs. You may see shelled molluscs of many types (stay clear of cone shells!), and perhaps some shell-less snails, such as the fried egg and clumped nudibranches, or the brightly colored one inch long fuschia flatworm. This is a good way to enjoy the water when swell has stirred up sediment, as it looks good even in 20-foot vis conditions because you're so close.

The surge zone is rarely visited by divers, so you'll spot fish there they seldom see. Beautiful sailfin tangs, spotted surgeonfish, Christmas wrasses, bluefin trevallies and occasional big surge wrasses love the constant wave action of the surge zone. You must use extra caution here, as wave action can throw you against the coral or rocks. Remember that periodic sets of bigger swell are likely, so always have an exit strategy, and be careful to not be in a spot where big waves could trap you.

As you venture further out at the edges of many sites, you'll enter the area of deep dropoffs. Swimming along the steep rocky walls, you're likely to see pelagic fish, such as ulua, leatherbacks, spotted eagle rays, and even an occasional manta ray. Watch out for currents, as they are more common and can be faster as you near the points of a bay. Don't take an unplanned trip to Tahiti!

You are unlikely to see all the fish that live in Hawai'i in just one lifetime: but it's worth a try. Are you having fun yet?

Lahaina Area

The town of Lahaina nestled between the ocean and tall peaks of west Maui is picturesque and popular. Unless staying in town, you're unlikely to snorkel from Lahaina beaches since they don't really merit the effort to find free parking or the five dollar fee. Māla Wharf at the north end of town is a small site, but the best in this area and a great spot to see some turtles.

There are a number of public access paths marked on our map, so give them a try if you're nearby. Otherwise, you're most likely to come here for one of the many excursions available from the Lahaina Harbor. From this harbor you can whale watch, dive, snorkel, take a sunset cruise, or travel to Molokini, Lānaʻi, or Molokaʻi.

We highly recommend taking the ferry (called Expeditions) to Lānaʻi, where you can easily spend the whole day between snorkeling, swimming, eating, and perhaps even checking out the island by car. There are several excellent snorkeling sites both near the harbor and within an easy (5-minute) walk from Mānele Harbor. Take the first ferry of the day and return to the lights of Lahaina on the last. It's a great way to avoid the crowds. See page 174 for details about the Lānaʻi snorkeling sites. It's best to check on water conditions if you want to count on good snorkeling on Lānaʻi. Avoid days with big south swells, which are more frequent in the summer.

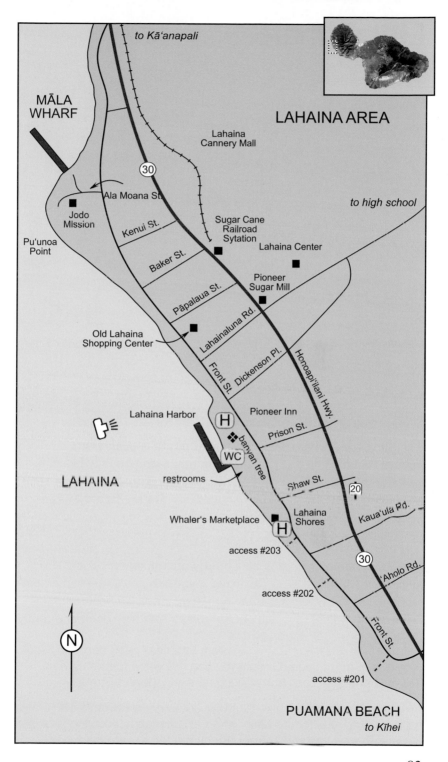

to Kā'anapali

MĀLA WHARF

LAHAINA AREA

Lahaina Cannery Mall

to high school

30

Ala Moana St.

Jodo Mission

Pu'unoa Point

Kenui St.

Sugar Cane Railroad Sytation

Lahaina Center

Baker St.

Pioneer Sugar Mill

Pāpalaua St.

Lahainaluna Rd.

Old Lahaina Shopping Center

Front St.

Dickenson Pl.

Honoapi'ilani Hwy.

Lahaina Harbor

H

Pioneer Inn

Prison St.

WC

banyan tree

LAHAINA

restrooms

Shaw St.

20

Whaler's Marketplace

Lahaina Shores

H

Kaua'ula Rd.

access #203

30

'Aholo Rd.

access #202

Front St.

N

access #201

PUAMANA BEACH
to Kīhei

Māla Wharf

This site offers better snorkeling than it might appear. There's usually enough parking and a small (and sometimes steep) sandy beach just south of the old pier. When the beach is calm, you can enter easily and snorkel near the pier to watch for baby sharks. To see lots of large turtles, head straight out to sea where you're sure to see them in the twenty-foot deep water.

Excursions sometimes stop here briefly after a snorkel elsewhere, so be alert for boats. They can avoid you easily in calm weather, but be more careful when swells are up. There's a small boat ramp just north of the wharf, so watch out for boats when they enter or exit.

GETTING THERE
From Lahaina, head north on Front Street (see map, page 83) until you see the signs to Māla Wharf. There is beach access and parking from Ala Moana Street.

From north of Lahaina, take Highway 30 south to Front Street. Watch on the ocean side for the Māla Wharf and beach access signs on Ala Moana. Restrooms and shower are on the left toward the wharf.

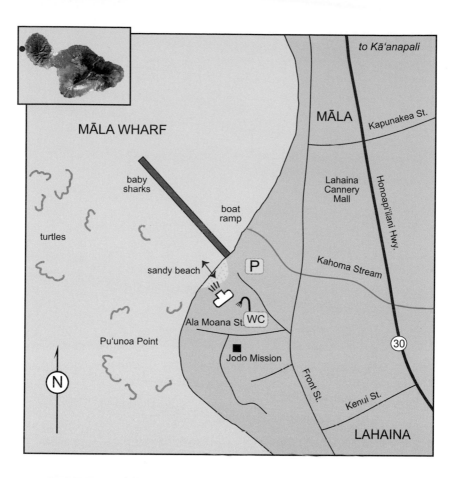

MĀLA WHARF

to Kāʻanapali

MĀLA

Kapunakea St.

baby sharks

boat ramp

Lahaina Cannery Mall

Honoapiʻilani Hwy.

turtles

sandy beach

Kahoma Stream

P

WC

Ala Moana St.

Puʻunoa Point

Jodo Mission

Front St.

Kenui St.

30

N

LAHAINA

octopus

Lahaina

While there is coral along the shore of the city of Lahaina, most of the area is usually rough and lacks much in the way of sand—making it better for surfing. Snorkeling is better at Māla Wharf at the north end of town or Puamana to the south.

Plenty of excursions and the ferry to Lānaʻi depart from the harbor, so you may find yourself looking for parking or restrooms. Street parking is mostly restricted to two hours, but small parking lots for pay are available scattered throughout the center of the city. These lots charge about $6 for all-day parking. Public restrooms are available near the center of the harbor-front, but are sometimes closed. When this happens, people use the ones at the Pioneer Inn. Be warned that you will need a quarter (exact change) to get in.

South of the city center, you'll find three public access paths to areas where there is a bit of sand as well as a bit of snorkeling, although certainly not the best.

GETTING THERE   Heading south on Front Street from the center of Lahaina, watch for the little blue public access signs. Just past Lahaina Shores you'll see access #203, a gravel path that goes fifty yards to the sand. Next south comes access #202 with a forty-yard concrete walkway. Just before Puamana, access #201 provides a twenty-yard path to the sand (see area map, page 83).

arc-eye hawkfish

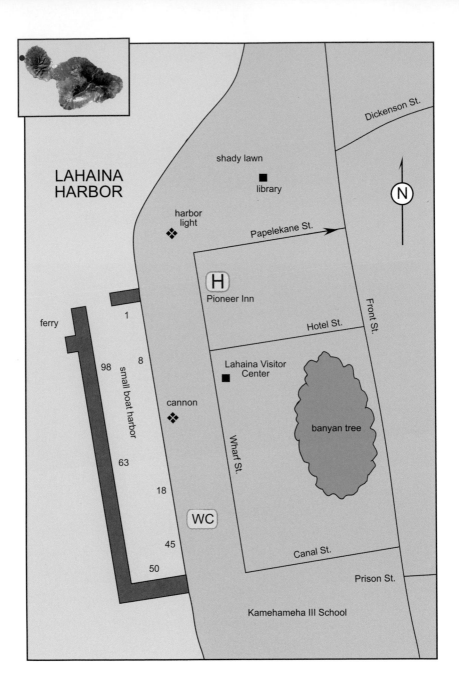

LAHAINA
HARBOR

shady lawn

■ library

harbor light

Papelekane St.

H Pioneer Inn

ferry

1

98

8

small boat harbor

cannon

63

18

45

50

Dickenson St.

N

Hotel St.

Front St.

Lahaina Visitor Center

banyan tree

Wharf St.

WC

Canal St.

Prison St.

Kamehameha III School

Puamana Beach Park

This little park is located just south of the housing area called Puamana. It has some sandy beach, some rocky shoreline, portapotties and picnic tables. While it's possible to snorkel here on a calm day, both swimming and snorkeling are better at most nearby parks. This one is best for surfing and picnics. A shower is located at the far north end of the park.

GETTING THERE   Going south on Highway 30 from Lahaina, Puamana is the first park just south of Lahaina where the highway angles in to the ocean (see map, page 83). There's parking and a small beach on the makai (Lahaina) side of Highway 30.

Olowalu Area

This southern section of West Maui offers a long string of public parks located in a narrow strip between Highway 30 and the sea. They are popular camping and picknicking spots with some stretches suitable to surfing, some for fishing and others for calm swimming and snorkeling.

There are no towns or hotels along here, but plenty of heavy traffic heading for Lahaina and north. Avoid rush hour if at all possible because it can be downright dangerous to make a left onto the highway in heavy traffic. You won't have the beach to yourself, but will leave the big crowds behind if you come early, or snorkel out a ways from the parks. Facilities are few with scattered portapotties, lots of picnic tables and thorny kiawe trees for shade. Most of these spots offer shallow water and a nice strip of sand making them popular family sites.

Parking is easy to find just off the highway makai. When storms kick up the swells, these beaches are often still calm since the large broad reef protects the shore. We continue with snorkeling sites in counterclockwise direction heading south from Lahaina. There is also some good snorkeling between Coral Gardens and Māʻalaea, but the climb down is difficult and entry is over rocks, so we don't recommend the area unless approached by boat.

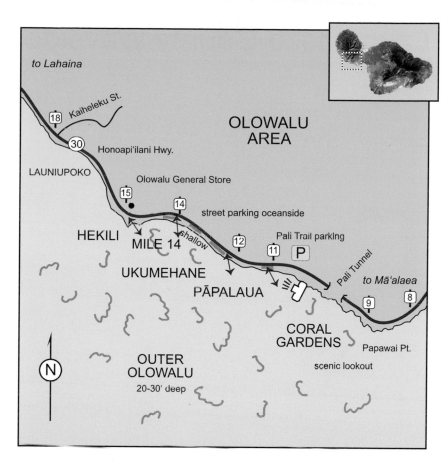

to Lahaina

Kaiheleku St.

18

30

Honoapi'ilani Hwy.

LAUNIUPOKO

OLOWALU
AREA

Olowalu General Store

15

14

street parking oceanside

HEKILI

MILE 14

shallow

12

11

Pali Trail parking

P

UKUMEHANE

PĀPALAUA

Pali Tunnel

to Mā'alaea

9

8

CORAL
GARDENS

Papawai Pt.

scenic lookout

N

OUTER
OLOWALU

20-30' deep

reef squid

Launiupoko County Wayside

Just north of mile marker 18 on Highway 30 you'll find this popular beach park. The waves are usually big enough for surfing, but a calm shallow kiddie pool is formed by the breakwater located in the center of the park.

You'll find plenty of grass, parking, restrooms, showers, picnic tables, shade trees and a little sand. The south end of the park is the best entry for some modest snorkeling. Picnicking and surfing here are the main attractions, as well as some kayak surfing.

GETTING THERE   Between Lahaina and Olowalu, this park is located along the ocean side of Highway 30, one tenth of a mile north of mile marker 18 (see area map, page 91). There's a traffic light where Kai Hele Ku Street heads toward the new housing in the foothills opposite the park. Turn into the park and look for a parking spot as far south as possible to be near the sandy area. Directly in front of the park the waves are usually more suited to surfing. The kiddie pool area is too shallow for snorkeling.

Hekili Point

This certainly isn't nearly as rich a snorkeling spot as nearby Olowalu, but it is calm, shallow and easy. It also offers a chance to study small fish and small coral heads. There's actually plenty going on in this shallow area. You can view the rice coral where beautiful green-eyed boxfish hang out. Watch the sandy bottom for the well-disguised octopus or flounder. You'll see plenty of tiny versions of your favorite fish since this shallow area (less than five feet deep within the protected area) is a good fish nursery.

GETTING THERE
On Highway 30 watch for the Olowalu General Store and mile marker 15 (see site map, page 95), and turn toward the ocean right across from the store. Then take an immediate left rather than straight. Follow this dirt road as it curves back toward the ocean and soon dead-ends in the small dirt parking area. A short path takes you to the ocean where you can see an old wharf to the left of the breakwater. Between them is a tiny sandy boat launching corridor where you can enter the water with ease. There are no facilities here.

Snorkel to the left anywhere within the protecting outer reef. It's an interesting opportunity to see juvenile fish—some exact scaled-down replicas of their parents, others with wildly different markings and shapes. When seas are very calm you can snorkel beyond the edge of the shallow inner reef.

Olowalu Beach (Mile 14)

Olowalu Beach is a very long beach with an extensive area of decent snorkeling. The reef here isn't as healthy as it used to be, but still has plenty of interesting coral and fish if you wander a bit. There are times when it's so milky that you can hardly see your hand in front of your face. Other days it's quite clear, with no obvious reason for the change. Brown algae and silt covers some of the coral, but this gradually lessens as you head away from shore.

The most famous spot is called Mile 14, since it's near that highway marker. This large, almost always calm, easy snorkeling area has something for everyone when the water is clear. Its long stretch of soft white sand has plenty of shade trees, parking and easy entry points. Beginners and children can stay close to shore if they wish.

Stronger swimmers and more experienced snorkelers can weave around the extensive reefs for about a mile straight out to sea, left or right. The coral here is large, but some is less healthy these days. When clear there are plenty of fish in every direction and it could hardly be easier as long as it is calm, which is almost year round. This reef extends far out to sea and usually offers protection from the surf. Parking is no problem at all. You'll see cars parked along the highway the whole length of the beach.

94

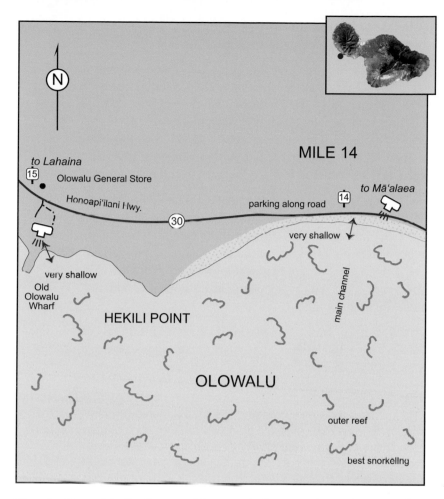

You don't need to limit yourself to snorkeling out the main channel noted on the map, unless you prefer a twenty-foot wide channel to head out through the coral, or the tide is very low. There are plenty of passages through the reef and you can safely swim over most of the coral unless the tide is unusually low or the swell is high. When the sea is calm, even a beginner would have no problem finding an easy passage. If you like plenty of clearance, just arrive near high tide.

We've been to Olowalu when it was clear near shore, but other times visibility was less than five feet. Brown algae can sometimes make for poor snorkeling near shore, as it covers up and crowds out the coral. Clean, healthy coral and visibility increase as you head out toward the outer, deeper reef. Experienced snorkelers can swim nearly a mile to what is called the Olowalu Outer Reef—assuming

95

calm conditions. Beginners will enjoy getting beyond the first section of reef just to marvel at the size of the coral.

This entire snorkeling area has coral 3-25 feet below the surface. You will see dramatic formations with large coral heads. Watch for most of Hawai'i's varied butterflyfish (lots of pairs of pretty ovals, teardrops and ornates). We have seen plenty of colorful parrotfish, groups of raccoon butterflyfish lined up in a row, lots of turtles, cornetfish, trumpetfish, boxfish with green eyes. Near shore we've seen the less common Picasso triggerfish and pearl wrasse.

This is a pretty picnic spot and great for small children who just want to splash in the calm water. Since the reef is so close to shore, this isn't the best spot for swimming. Take care how far out you snorkel when waves are breaking on the outer edge of the reef. No facilities are located here, except that portapotties are scattered along this section of coast. You'll find some at Ukumehame Beach Park, the next site to the south.

And a word of warning about the kiawe trees lining this beach. The long, sharp kiawe thorns lay in wait in the sand, so wear your flip-flops and puncture them instead of your feet.

GETTING THERE
Just south of the Olowalu General Store across from mile marker 14 is an extensive area for snorkeling (see map, page 95). There's plenty of parking on the makai (ocean) side of the highway, with shade available under the kiawe trees. You'll see clusters of cars at popular spots. You might want to try the center first, then return another day to explore this exceptionally broad reef area. The wide channel is located about fifty feet south of marker 14 and appears light green in contrast to the darker reef area.

Getting back on the highway here is often hazardous due to the steady streams of traffic in both directions. First, drive on the gravel area to one of the sections with either an asphalt verge, or not too severe a dropoff from the pavement. Then be patient until you get a safe opportunity—it can take awhile. Remember when we told you that driving to the beach was a lot riskier than snorkeling?

Discounts

Discounts are available for many excursions. If you're so inclined, a little work and the right questions can save you a fair chunk of change. Begin by picking up one of the numerous free promotional magazines such as Maui Gold. These are readily available at the airport, hotels and shops. They usually include special offers, coupons and other deals to attract customers.

Calling an excursion office and asking if there are any special offers can sometimes pay off, especially when tourism is slower. Summer and holidays the ships fill more quickly, but there is still plenty of competition on Maui, so it's always worth a try.

Ships often charge less for children and nothing for toddlers. Each ship has its own definition of child and adult. Don't hesitate to ask about senior discounts, repeat customer discounts, and kama'āina rate (if you live in the islands and can prove it by showing your driver's license). Sometimes discounts are provided to AAA members.

For discounts ranging from 10-20%, try Activity Warehouse in Lahaina.

If you have a browser, try: www.travelhawaii.com

It helps to have a flexible schedule and be able to go on short notice.

For a free trip, sign up for a timeshare offer. You will have to sit through an hour or two of sales talk in exchange for your bargain trip. Do not underestimate their sales ability!

When you do book tickets ahead of time and charge them to your credit card, remember that when the ship goes out with or without you, you will be charged for the trip. The fine print usually requires you to cancel at least 24 hours ahead. You may wake up to weather that doesn't suit you only to find that the ship sailed anyway, and you will get to pay as agreed. Also, your destination isn't guaranteed. You might have your heart set on Molokini Island only to find the ship change to Coral Gardens due to rough weather in the channel. This does not entitle you to cancel at no charge. Keep in mind they only make changes for true safety reasons, so go with the flow and trust your captain.

Ukumehame Beach Park

This small beach park south of Olowalu is slightly less protected than it, so not as calm. There is a sandy beach here, but is too shallow and rocky for comfortable snorkeling, and can be quite windy. It does have portable toilets which some snorkel sites lack. You'll find picnic tables here, but not a lot of shade. This park seems to also catch more of the south swell than nearby Olowalu.

GETTING THERE   Between Olowalu and Pāpalaua on Highway 30, you'll see this park by the highway on the makai (ocean) side (see area map, page 91), between mile markers 12 and 13.

Pāpalaua Park (Coral Gardens)

Just south of Ukumehame is another of the small parks along the makai (ocean) side of Highway 30 between Olowalu and the Pali Tunnel. Located at mile marker 11, it provides a good entry point for snorkeling to Coral Gardens, a popular snorkel excursion destination. The best spot to enter is from the small sandy beach at the south end of the park. Snorkel out to sea and toward the south to see the area called Coral Gardens (see map, page 91). When the sea is calm,

98

snorkel about 300 yards from shore to see large healthy coral heads spread over a wide area. You won't see as many fish here as other sites, but the coral is worth a trip. The reef is 3-15 feet deep all the way making for good viewing. Our favorite spot is directly out to sea from the trail head marked on our map.

Coral Gardens can also be reached from the highway further south— from the Lahaina Pali Trail parking area across the highway. There isn't a sandy entry there, just rocky shore. Also it's a scramble down the side of the hill.

There are no facilities here other than portable toilets towards the north and parking along the sand.

GETTING THERE
Watch for mile markers to know which of the little seaside parks will access Coral Gardens (see area map, page 91). Pāpalaua Park is the closest.

From Lahaina go south on Highway 30 until you see mile marker 11. This is six tenths of a mile north of the Pali Tunnel. Park at the southern end of the long park and enter from the small sandy beach, swimming out and south to explore this extensive reef.

From Kīhei head north to Highway 30. After emerging from the Pali Tunnel, drive six tenths of a mile more to the little park on the makai (ocean) side of the highway. Park as close as you can to the south end of the park.

Kīhei Area

The Kīhei area offers plenty of condos and sand. The pretty sand beach area is about six miles long with some rocky points along the way, so there's ample room to swim and sun. These beaches mostly have good public facilities including parking, restrooms and showers. Water quality is probably better as you head south. We prefer to stay out of the water until at least as far south as Kalama Beach Park. Each park has very limited parking, so this can be a problem midday or on weekends. People do come and go often, so you're likely to find a spot eventually.

The town itself has lots of markets, shopping, banks and restaurants. This can be a cooler part of Maui in the summer because the winds often blow across this low area between Maui's high mountains. Kīhei offers a wide range of condos (some quite inexpensive) and the area is convenient for excursions around the island, so it's not a bad base for snorkelers as long as you don't expect to snorkel in front of your condo all the time. We prefer to be located a bit outside the town to avoid the crowds. The broad stretches of sand and fairly calm water make this a popular spot for families with young children. The condos at either end of town are more likely to be quiet. Of course, they are also likely to be a bit more expensive. We prefer the south to be closer to the best snorkeling.

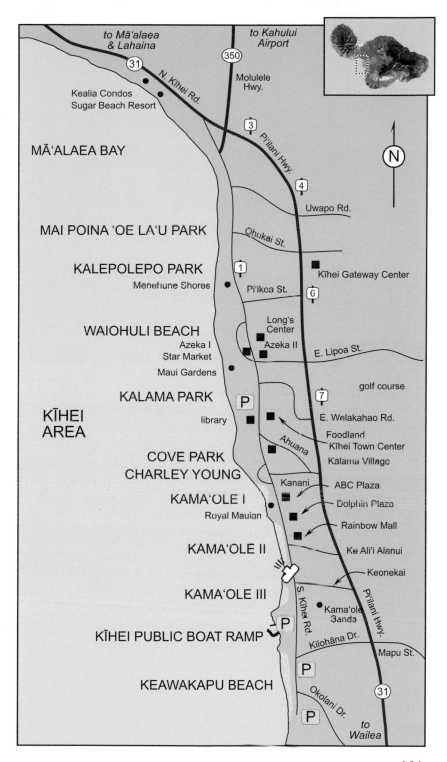

to Māʻalaea
& Lahaina

to Kahului
Airport

31

350

N. Kīhei Rd.

Molulele
Hwy.

Kealia Condos
Sugar Beach Resort

Piʻilani Hwy.

3

MĀʻALAEA BAY

N

4

Uwapo Rd.

MAI POINA ʻOE LAʻU PARK

Ohukai St.

KALEPOLEPO PARK

1

Kīhei Gateway Center

Menehune Shores

Piʻikea St.

6

WAIOHULI BEACH

Longʻs
Center

Azeka I

Azeka II

Star Market

E. Lipoa St.

Maui Gardens

KALAMA PARK

golf course

KĪHEI
AREA

P

7

E. Welakahao Rd.

library

Ahuana

Foodland
Kīhei Town Center

COVE PARK

Kalama Village

CHARLEY YOUNG

Kanani

ABC Plaza

KAMAʻOLE I

Dolphin Plaza

Royal Mauian

Rainbow Mall

KAMAʻOLE II

Ke Aliʻi Alanui

Keonekai

KAMAʻOLE III

S. Kīhei Rd.

Piʻilani Hwy.

Kamaʻole
Sands

KĪHEI PUBLIC BOAT RAMP

P

Kilohāna Dr.

Mapu St.

P

31

KEAWAKAPU BEACH

Okolani Dr.

to
Wailea

P

Māʻalaea Harbor

While not a snorkeling destination, Māʻalaea Harbor does offer numerous excursions to Molokini and various sites along this coast. Many excursions offer morning and afternoon trips with the afternoon cheaper, however, the ocean tends to be calmer in the morning. On a completely calm day, there is little difference, but there are plenty of days when the afternoon trip can be quite uncomfortable—especially if you're prone to sea sickness (check page 21 for remedies). The harbor parking lot is a bit too small when lots of boats are heading out, but there are plenty of alternatives within an easy walk.

The Maui Ocean Center is well worth a visit. It is located behind the harbor with plenty of parking. It features Hawaiʻian fish, coral and mammals. Everything from sea jellies, eels, butterflyfish, to sharks and rays. Exhibits are both inside and out, so bring sunglasses and hat. There is an excellent gift shop in case you want something to take to the folks back home.

We don't recommend snorkeling or swimming along this section of the coast because the water here has had pollution problems in the past. It improves beginning in mid-Kīhei, and is probably even better as you head further south.

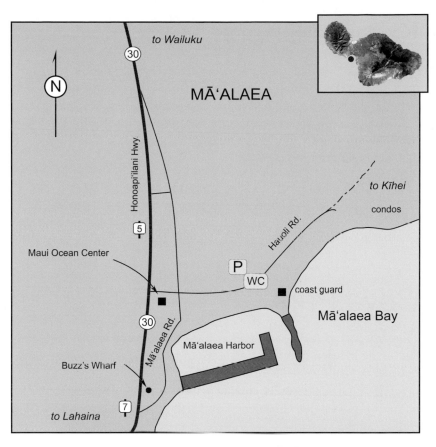

MĀʻALAEA

to Wailuku

30

N

Honoapiʻilani Hwy

5

Maui Ocean Center

30

Buzzʼs Wharf

7

to Lahaina

to Kīhei

condos

Hauoli Rd.

P

WC

coast guard

Māʻalaea Bay

Māʻalaea Rd.

Māʻalaea Harbor

raccoon butterflyfish

Kalama Beach Park

This large and popular park has room for everyone and is often calm enough for safe swimming and a bit of snorkeling. There's plenty of parking, grass, soft sand, restrooms and picnic tables, however, not really much to see underwater. Still, when calm, it's a good place to learn how to snorkel. It's also a nice spot for children with a large play area and shallow, calm water.

GETTING THERE   Located in the center of Kīhei along South Kīhei Road, this large park is easy to find. From Highway 31, take the Lipoa exit (see area map, page 101) and continue south on South Kīhei Road.

Cove Park

This tiny park is tucked in a corner between Kalama Beach Park and Kamaʻole I Beach Park. It offers a bit of sand and a very pretty view, but parking isn't easy. There's a bit of snorkeling too, but not really much to see. Unless you're staying within walking distance, don't bother to snorkel here since coral and fish are more numerous further south.

GETTING THERE   Driving south on South Kīhei Road, continue past Kalama Park and Shores of Maui, then watch carefully or you'll miss it (see area map, page 101).

Charley Young Beach Park

This pretty little spot offers a sandy beach, no crowds and even has a shower. Parking, however, isn't great—with just three spaces. It's a nice place for a swim and a shower. Snorkeling is possible, but there generally isn't much to see near shore.

GETTING THERE   Between Cove Park and Kam I, this beach is hidden at the end of Kaiʻau Place (off South Kīhei Road). If you take this road toward the ocean, you'll see the little blue beach access sign (see map, page 101).

Kama'ole I Beach Park

The next three beaches are all in a row on the makai side of South Kīhei Road. They offer sandy beaches, lovely views, boogie boarding, and good swimming most of the year. You can walk the full length of all three by climbing up and over the small rocky points that separate them. They are popular spots for sunning, swimming, playing and enjoying the sunset. Snorkeling here is possible when calm, but there really isn't a lot to see. These parks do provide good sites to learn how to snorkel and you'll see scattered coral heads with some very pretty fish. All three of the Kam parks provide parking, restrooms, showers, lifeguards, grass, shade and plenty of sand.

GETTING THERE   Kam I, II and III are well-marked along South Kīhei Road south of the center of Kīhei (see map, page 101). All offer some parking, grass, shade, soft sandy beaches and restrooms. The beaches are usually relatively calm, but not flat. Waves can pick up along this section of Maui when there is south swell (usually in the summer), so head elsewhere on the island if this is a problem. Afternoons tend to be a bit choppy too—especially when it get windy, so try to snorkel or swim before noon for the calmest conditions. Sometimes late afternoon gets very calm again.

Kamaʻole II Beach Park

This next beach immediately to the south is known as Kam II. It's nearly identical to the other Kams, but has one important amenity—a bigger parking lot. The lot (along with most in the area) is open 7 a.m. till 7 p.m., then the gates are locked. Snorkeling is modest, but OK for a beginner. South swells in the summer can discourage a beginner, but early morning is often calm enough.

Kamaʻole III Beach Park

Kam III is probably the prettiest of the Kam beaches with more canopy trees for shade. Snorkeling gets a bit better as we head south, but still only modest compared to further south. Better suited for swimming and boogie boarding, but not a bad site for learning how to snorkel—especially in the early morning. Snorkel toward either of the rocky points and a bit out to sea when the swells aren't high. Sometimes late afternoon brings calm water again. High wind makes for choppy conditions—not what beginners need.

Kīhei Boat Ramp

Since the public boat ramp provides a small breakwater and has a small sandy beach on the right (to the north), this is an easy entry point for snorkeling in the south Kīhei area. The boat ramp is quite busy during the day (with trips to Molokini and elsewhere), so you might prefer to enter through a narrow channel just south of the breakwater where you won't encounter any boats. The snorkeling here is good when calm enough to head straight out where the water is about 10-20 feet deep. You do have to watch out for boats entering the ramp area— especially when the swells are high enough to hide a snorkeler. This is another excellent spot to see turtles, especially in the deeper areas. Excursions often stop offshore here to check out the turtles after a trip to Molokini. They call this site Turtle Town. Visibility is usually only about 30 feet and it tends to be a bit choppy, but you still won't miss the turtles.

GETTING THERE From Kīhei, take South Kīhei Road until you see the boat ramp on the ocean side of the road (see area map, page 101). You'll find a parking lot with plenty of space, grassy area with trees, picnic tables as well as restrooms and a shower.

Keawakapu Beach Park

This long, skinny park stretches along a mile of sandy beach just south of Kīhei. There are three public accesses (#108, #109 and #110) with three parking lots, although all are easy to miss (see map, page 109). The central access offers better parking and a shower, but no other facilities. This is a nice spot for families to enjoy the sand, calm water and lovely view. Snorkeling is best from the south access where you can snorkel toward the left. The water in front of the beach park is all rather shallow with a fair amount of scattered rocks (mediocre snorkeling and swimming). The snorkeling here is a bit better than most of Kīhei and the parking much easier. Portapotties are located at both ends of the park, a shower only in the middle.

GETTING THERE
From Kīhei, take South Kīhei Rd. This dead-ends at the southern access to Keawakapu. See map, page 109 for more information about the three public accesses. Heading south on Highway 31, turn right on Kilohana Drive, which will take you to a parking lot for Keawakapu Beach at the corner of South Kīhei Road. Walk from here to the center of the beach and to the only shower. This is access #109. See map, page 109.

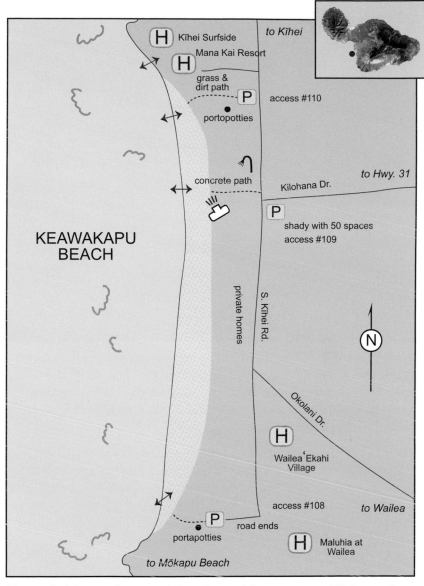

KEAWAKAPU
BEACH

Kīhei Surfside
Mana Kai Resort
to Kīhei
grass &
dirt path
access #110
portopotties
concrete path
Kilohana Dr.
to Hwy. 31
shady with 50 spaces
access #109
private homes
S. Kīhei Rd.
N
Okolani Dr.
Wailea ʻEkahi
Village
access #108
to Wailea
road ends
portapotties
Maluhia at
Wailea
to Mōkapu Beach

To snorkel the northern part, turn toward the ocean on Kilohana, then go right at the end and park near the Mana Kai Resort. You'll see the public access path, but public parking is more confusing. We park on the outer edge of the dirt parking lot, leaving the closer spaces for the resort. There is a good entry in front of the Kīhei Surfside. Snorkel either direction.

To get to the southern (and best) end of Keawakapu, follow Kīhei Rd. to the south as far as possible, then turn right into the gravel parking area, access #108. Snorkel to the left around the point (south).

Wailea Area

The western coast of South Maui has been growing rapidly in recent years. This is a beautiful area located in the rain shadow of Haleakala with views of several islands off the coast. Huge hotels of various styles have been built on terrific beaches. Other equally nice beaches remain secluded for the time being.

There are relatively few condos here (but most are excellent) and prices are usually high. Hotel styles and sizes vary, so select a hotel according to your taste and budget, or choose a good beach and settle for what accommodations are there. This is really a great place for snorkelers, from beginners to advanced. It's not quite as calm as the little bays in West Maui, but it has plenty of coves, points, pretty beaches and lava fields.

With reef extending far out to sea, Wailea hosts lots of turtles and interesting pelagic fish. All in all, an excellent location for serious snorkelers. If the prices are too steep for your pocketbook, stay in the Kīhei area and drive here to snorkel.

As Wailea becomes more and more popular, Highway 31 will probably eventually be extended and connected with Highway 37, but people have been waiting for this a long time. There are side roads that connect, but all are private at the moment.

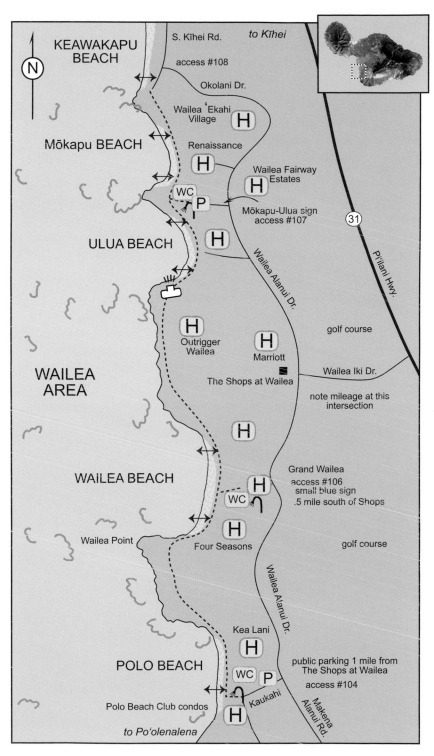

KEAWAKAPU BEACH

S. Kīhei Rd.

to Kīhei

access #108

Okolani Dr.

Wailea ʻEkahi Village

Mōkapu BEACH

Renaissance

Wailea Fairway Estates

Mōkapu-Ulua sign
access #107

31

Pʻilani Hwy.

ULUA BEACH

WC P

WAILEA AREA

Outrigger Wailea

Marriott

golf course

The Shops at Wailea

Wailea Iki Dr.

note mileage at this intersection

Wailea Alanui Dr.

WAILEA BEACH

Grand Wailea
access #106
small blue sign
.5 mile south of Shops

WC

Wailea Point

Four Seasons

golf course

Wailea Alanui Dr.

Kea Lani

POLO BEACH

WC P

public parking 1 mile from
The Shops at Wailea

access #104

Polo Beach Club condos

Kaukahi

Makena Alanui Rd.

to Poʻolenalena

The beaches of Wailea offer broad soft sand, usually calm snorkeling, and gorgeous views of nearby islands. On a clear day you can see West Maui, Lānaʻi, Kahoʻolawe, Puʻu Olaʻi (Red Hill), and Molokini.

We continue now with snorkeling sites along the whole Wailea coast heading south from Keawakapu Beach Park to Maluaka Beach. Since Molokini Island is close by, we include it at the end of the Wailea Area sites.

Snorkeling is best here before noon, when the cool breezes pick up making the water choppy and sometimes even dangerous. With chop snorkels, we don't mind the wind-driven choppy conditions as long as the waves and currents don't pick up too much. Beginners are likely to prefer mornings—the earlier, the better.

Parking is also much easier early in the day since the public lots aren't large and this is a very popular section of coast. This is particularly true for weekends and holidays. Most parking lots are open from 7 a.m. till around 7 p.m. If you stay longer than the posted time, expect to find your car trapped behind locked gates. Also, avoid parking illegally because the ever-present and growing security patrols may ticket you.

Mōkapu Beach

Mōkapu Beach

If you manage to find a parking space in the Ulua/Mōkapu public lot, Mōkapu Beach is to the north of the point near the lot, while Ulua Beach is to the south. You can snorkel from Ulua Beach north completely around the point or, just to be different, you can begin your snorkel at Mōkapu and end up at Ulua—assuming you plan to snorkel the whole point. It would be too far for most beginners, but is quite easy for an intermediate snorkeler. This makes an excellent one-way snorkel if you walk back on the beach path provided by the hotels. Mornings are the calmest time for snorkeling out past the point. The coral and numbers of fish increase as you head out to deeper water (about fifteen feet deep). While you'll find coral and fish near shore, you won't find large numbers. Avoid the outer points when larger swell arrives—especially south swell in the summer. And stay along the edge rather than crossing the reef when any big swell might drag you over the coral.

Swimming is great here since there is a large sandy beach at both Mōkapu and Ulua with relatively calm conditions. It can, however, get rough, especially when large south swells arrive from the southern hemisphere. Local winds can also cause large enough waves to discourage swimmers, especially in the afternoon. It's easier for a swimmer to cope with waves because a swimmer can see them coming. Snorkelers need to be aware of water rising, dropping, or surging—indicating a change.

GETTING THERE   Take Highway 31 south past Kīhei and turn right on Wailea Iki Drive at the end of the highway (see area map, page 111). At the end of Wailea Iki Drive, turn right on Wailea Alanui Drive and watch for the small green sign that says Mōkapu-Ulua Beach (access #107). It's easy to miss—on the makai side of the road, across from the Wailea Fairway Estates. The beach sign used to be large and prominent!

You'll find parking, showers, restrooms, picnic tables, a grassy hill and shade. Come early if you want a parking spot near the beach. Mōkapu is the beach just to the north of this beautiful point. So Mōkapu is on your right, while Ulua is in front. This stretch of beaches in front of the big hotels all connects by a walkway that extends from Mōkapu Beach to Polo Beach. It's all beautiful, but seldom uncrowded—especially on those ever-common dazzling sunny days.

Ulua Beach Park

At this very popular snorkeling and shore diving spot, you can snorkel around the point to the right or far out to sea as well. Coral and fish are plentiful. This beach is best snorkeled before the afternoon winds arrive. Picnic on the grassy hill at the north end of the beach and enjoy the gorgeous view. All amenities are available.

This is a very popular spot, so come early or late if you want to avoid crowds (before 9 a.m. or after 3 p.m.). Experienced snorkelers can easily swim beyond the crowd of beginners who tend to stay close to shore. This is an excellent site, with lots to see, a beautiful setting, and a reasonable amount of parking. When calm, it's easy to snorkel around the point to Mōkapu Beach. In fact, a good swimmer can snorkel all the way to Keawakapu Beach Park. A beach walkway connects all these beaches, making a one-way snorkel simple. You can also snorkel quite a ways out to sea where turtles are common in twenty feet of water.

Most of the water is only about ten feet deep with scattered patches of reef that extend well beyond the point. You're likely to see some of the green sea turtles in this area as well as schools of reef fish.

Large numbers of turtles hang out on the reef further from shore—especially where the reef drops down to twenty feet deep. The sea here is usually calmest in the morning with swells picking up around noon. Stay on the edge of the reef if swells get big enough to scrape you along the coral. Swimming is excellent here along the sandy beach, but usually better in the mornings before wind-driven swells make it more exciting.

GETTING THERE

Ulua is the beach in front of the Wailea Beach Resort, with lots of big resorts nearby (see area map, page 111). Take Highway 31 south past Kīhei and watch for Wailea Iki Dri. to the right heading toward the resorts. At The Shops at Wailea turn right on Wailea Alanui Rd. toward the Wailea Beach Resort. On your left you'll quickly see a small green sign for Mōkapu/Ulua Beach across from the Wailea Fairway Estates. This is public access #107. Drop people and gear at the beach near the showers and restrooms, then send the driver off to locate a parking spot.

As Ulua becomes ever more popular, you will need to arrive earlier in the morning for space, but that's nearly always the best time to snorkel here. You'll avoid the crowds and the wind-driven choppy water. Don't try to park illegally because these popular parking lots are heavily patrolled.

Wailea Beach

Snorkeling is best at the south end of Wailea beach toward the point. Early in the day it's usually calmer, while the wind typically picks up by noon making for choppy conditions. When calm, this beach offers good snorkeling further out. Swimming is great in the sandy middle.

You're almost sure to see turtles if you stay in the water for awhile. Please remember they are protected by Hawai'ian law, so don't touch them, hover over them or chase them. The reef here extends about a mile toward the sea and is shallow enough for snorkeling most of the way out. Stay closer to shore if it gets choppy or you begin to encounter a strong current.

On calm days, we have seen many turtles, a snowflake eel, numerous large tangs, needlefish, red pencil urchins as well as the usual reef dwellers. The public access offers parking, restrooms and showers. You'll enjoy the dramatic view on a clear Maui day.

GETTING THERE   This beach is between the Grand Hyatt Wailea Resort to the south, and the Four Seasons Hotel to the north (see area map, page 111). From Highway 31, turn right on Wailea Iki Drive, then left on Wailea Alanui Road at The Shops at Wailea to the first public access (#106). Watch carefully for a small blue public access sign (easy to miss!) and turn right between the Grand Wailea and the Four Seasons hotels. Here you'll find a parking lot for about 50 cars, then another for about 20, followed by restrooms and showers. Take the path directly to the beach. From the sand, snorkel to the left towards the point and around if calm enough. Swimming is excellent over sand in the middle.

If You Love the Reef

- Show respect for the reef creatures by causing them no harm.

- Avoid touching or standing on the coral, as touching kills it.

- Come as a respectful visitor rather than as a predator.

- Leave the many beautiful creatures you find there in peace so that others may enjoy them as you have.

- Allow the fish their usual diet rather than feeding them. Feeding them ultimately destroys their natural balance, and causes their numbers to decline. It also makes them more aggressive towards people, and can result in fish bites.

- Global warming is gradually damaging reefs around the globe, so it's even more important to keep Hawai'ian reefs healthy. Do a part by minimizing spillage of any chemicals that may wind up draining onto the reef.

- Join our reef Easter egg hunt: try to find and dive for at least one piece of trash on every snorkel, and take it away with you. It sharpens your eye, and if enough folks do it, it will be hard to find any. Don't try to clean up the whole world. Just pick up one or two things every time you're out. This includes fishing line and sinkers.

- Use sunscreen less, and cover-ups more. Sunscreen dissolves in the water, and is toxic to fish and coral. A lycra body suit or a wetsuit takes care of most of your body anyway, and for your sensitive face, or wear a big hat. It's one of the best gifts you can give the reef.

Polo Beach Park

While Polo is a very attractive beach, it's not the very best snorkeling or swimming in Wailea. Still, it's OK and you'll find public access, adequate parking and excellent facilities. This is also a pleasant spot for a picnic. It's a popular vacation site for families.

Polo Beach is located between the huge white turrets of Kea Lani Hotel (which can't be missed, even if you close your eyes) and the tall Polo Beach Club building. The main drawback of this picturesque beach is that it's a little rocky with less clearance than the beaches to the north.

Strong swimmers can snorkel from here to Ulua or Wailea. The beach walkway will bring you back to Polo Beach. Since the beach here is a little more shallow than the rest of Wailea, you will probably prefer high tide. Swimming is definitely possible here, but better at the several beaches to the north. This narrow park has a path to the beach, restrooms, excellent shower, picnic tables, shade trees and a beautiful view of the neighboring islands. Mornings are almost always the best for calm water. Sometimes the breezes and chop calm down again in the late afternoon—just before sunset.

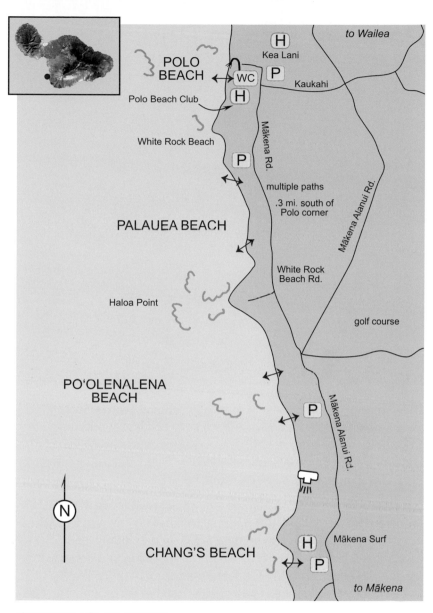

POLO
BEACH

to Wailea

H
Kea Lani

WC   P
Kaukahi

Polo Beach Club   H

White Rock Beach

Mākena Rd.

P

multiple paths
.3 mi. south of
Polo corner

PALAUEA BEACH

Mākena Alanui Rd.

White Rock
Beach Rd.

Haloa Point

golf course

PO'OLENALENA
BEACH

P

Mākena Alanui Rd.

N

Mākena Surf

CHANG'S BEACH   H
P

to Mākena

GETTING THERE   From Highway 31, take a right
toward Wailea, then a left on Wailea Alanui Road when you must turn
(see area map, page 111). From this corner, continue one mile south
on Wailea Alanui Road and right on Kaukahi to the public access for
Polo Beach parking. It's just past the main entrance to the Kea Lani
where you take a sharp turn to the right. You'll see a green sign at
the entrance to parking. All of these resort parking areas are heavily
patrolled, so stick with legal parking spaces.

Palauea Beach Park

By no means the prettiest spot in the exceptional Wailea/Mākena area, Palauea Beach Park does offer some excellent snorkeling. Swimming is good if you don't mind that the sandy beach stays about three feet deep for quite a ways out. That makes it nice for little kids though.

This 500-foot long park along the side of the road is lined with thorny kiawe trees, has a dirt parking area and no amenities—not even enough trash cans. Swimming is OK in the middle, and snorkeling is fine at either end. We prefer the south end because it usually has better visibility (30 feet rather than 20 in the north). Entry and exit are easy over the gently sloping sand at either end. The best snorkeling is found as you swim to the south around the point to an area in front of two lava and coral storm beaches. There we have seen about a dozen turtles, whitetip reef shark, Picasso triggerfish, and saddleback butterfly fish that are relatively rare on Maui.

Come early when the sea is calm and you may have this nice site entirely to yourself. Afternoon can bring swells that would make it difficult to swim out to the best stuff. A nice shower and restrooms are available just to the north at the Polo Beach Park.

GETTING THERE Go south on Highway 31, turning toward the ocean on Wailea Iki Drive, then left on Wailea Alanui Drive (see map, page 119). Go right on Kaukahi, then left on Mākena Road past Polo Beach. You'll find Palauea Beach begins about .3 of a mile south of Polo Beach. Park in the dirt area along the road and take any of the short multiple paths through the kiawe trees to the water. Where you park depends on which end you wish to snorkel.

juvenile rockmover wrasse

adult rockmover wrasse

Po'olenalena Beach Park

Heading south, Po'olenalena is the next (and similarly shallow) beach along the side of the road. Just a gravel parking area with one portapotty and a great place to step on one of those wicked kiawe thorns. There's also a fair amount of trash, so it isn't nearly as appealing on land as the manicured hotel beaches to the north.

We park at the north end of the beach and snorkel to the right around a modest point where we rapidly spotted three octopuses and many turtles. To spot a fascinating octopus you need what the locals call "tako eye" (tako is Japanese for octopus). Watch for that rock or coral piece that moves a little because tako can quickly imitate both the color and texture of sand, rock or coral. It's wonderful to have a chance to see them moving about and changing both color and texture in a split second.

This is a small point, so not a place where you can wander very far. But, it's also usually quite safe. Swimming is good if you don't requite water deeper than about three feet. This beach stays shallow for quite a ways out to sea. The southern end of Po'olenalena Beach joins Chang's Beach, another good place to swim and snorkel.

122

GETTING THERE   From Wailea go south on Mākena Alanui Drive (see maps, pages 111 and 119). To get to the north end, jog right on Mākena Road and look for a sign with parking in a dirt lot on the ocean side of the road. You'll see the beach and portapotty from here. Walk carefully through the kiawe trees to the sand, then snorkel around the small point to your right (north). For the south end you may want to park along the road further south. An excellent shower and restrooms await at Polo Beach Park if you follow Mākena Road north to the lot just south of the Kea Lani— assuming you can find a parking spot.

Disposable Cameras

Cheap, widely available, even stocked on some excursions, and fun to use. Keep your expectations realistic and you won't end up disappointed, although don't expect to get pictures like you see in National Geographic. The professionals who get all those great shots use camera setups worth $10,000 and more. They also have assistants underwater to hold the lights and spare cameras. Their books start to look like bargains compared with trying to get these pictures by yourself! Check out the great selection of marine life books in Maui bookstores.

Still, it's fun to try for that cute shot of your sweetie in a bikini, clowning with the fish. If you're lucky, you'll actually have identifiable fish in a few shots. The cameras won't focus closer than about four feet, so the fish will look much smaller than you remember them. These cameras work best when it's sunny with good visibility and the subject fish as close as the camera allows.

They do work OK above the water too, and so make a great knock-around camera to haul around wet or dry without paranoia about theft, saltwater or damage. Try a picture of the beautiful mountains of West Maui as you float in the calm waters of Honolua Bay.

An interesting alternative to disposable cameras are the new moderate cost digital cameras rated to work up to 5 to 10 feet deep without any waterproof housing. They do work, and can take decent pictures, definitely a cut above disposable cameras. We have heard comments that they are prone to flooding (leaking) if you either go a little too deep, or push them too quickly through the water, which is the equivalent of taking them deeper. If you have the budget, you might try them.

Chang's Beach (Mākena Surf)

Chang's Beach at the Mākena Surf condos is an easily-missed, but delightful, beach with excellent safe swimming and snorkeling. The beach is entirely surrounded by the two-story Mākena Surf condos, but good public access is provided, if you arrive early and watch carefully for the little blue sign. No public facilities are available except a shower.

This beach is really a small gem and is one of our Maui favorites. It combines a pretty and serene beach, hard to beat easy access from sand for swimming and good snorkeling in a calm bay. When south swell arrive, this beach is calmer than most in the area because the sand slopes so gently making for easier waves.

As usual in Maui on an exposed beach, waves and swell can really pick up after noon, so come early to avoid choppy water. The large, deluxe condos are available for rent, and make a great family base if the hefty rental rates are within your budget. The small public parking lot is open from 7 a.m. till 20 minutes past sunset, then the yellow gate will be locked.

GETTING THERE
Go south on Highway 31, turning right toward Wailea on Wailea Iki Drive, then left on Wailea Alanui Road when you come to the big shopping center and have to turn one way or the other (see area map, page 119). Continue south for

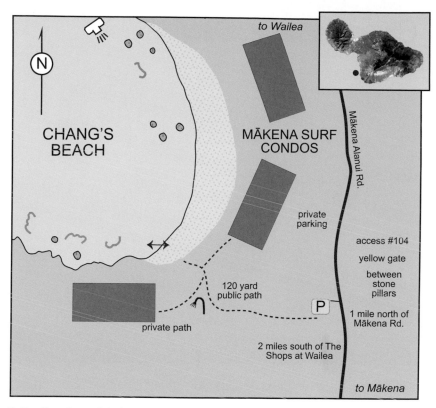

Map labels:
- to Wailea
- N
- CHANG'S BEACH
- MĀKENA SURF CONDOS
- Mākena Alanui Rd.
- private parking
- access #104
- yellow gate
- between stone pillars
- 120 yard public path
- P
- 1 mile north of Mākena Rd.
- private path
- 2 miles south of The Shops at Wailea
- to Mākena

3.5 miles from this intersection. Watch for the rock walls surrounding the Mākena Surf. There is a small entrance to a nine-car public parking lot with a little blue "public access #104" sign posted in an inconspicuous spot, near the main entrance to the condos.

The paved, shady trail starts at the front left of the parking lot where you will go through a gate. Just follow the winding trail downhill through the flowers to the beach. Snorkel the left side of the beach, just steps from the end of the path.

Finding your way back up to your car can be the hardest part. It's all too easy to wander off on one of the side trails that dead-end at sections of the condos. From the beach, the trail leads straight to a Y. Be sure to angle right here. Go left at the next Y and you'll find the shower on your right. Check our map first. If you end up in the wrong parking lot, you won't even be able to get out to the street due to the gates, so you'll have to double back almost to the beach.

A shower and restrooms are available if you follow the coast back north to the Polo Beach Park, although you may not find any parking in the middle of the day—especially on weekends. The parking near the big hotels is heavily patrolled, so don't park here illegally.

Five Graves/Caves

This popular area includes several entries ranging in difficulty from beginner to advanced and is often snorkeled by boat access. There are plenty of turtles in the area as well as interesting canyons and coves. It's often a better site for scuba than for snorkeling when conditions are a little rougher and the entrance is challenging. It has a tendency to be choppy as well as murky, but still worth checking out for a vast area to explore.

On a nice day it can make for very enjoyable snorkeling, especially when the visibility is good enough to see the turtles. They often rest on the bottom, where it is fifteen to twenty feet deep. Look sharp in sandy pockets among the coral and you'll be rewarded. Unless the sea is completely calm, be careful of the lava entrance here since it's narrow and sharp. You don't want some sudden swells scraping you against the lava.

The area straight out to sea (Turtle Town) is where many of the excursions stop to see turtles on their return from Molokini. You can actually snorkel that far, but you must be watchful for the boats—especially if swell is high enough that a boat might not see you. The nearest facilities and plenty of parking are located at nearby Mākena Landing Park.

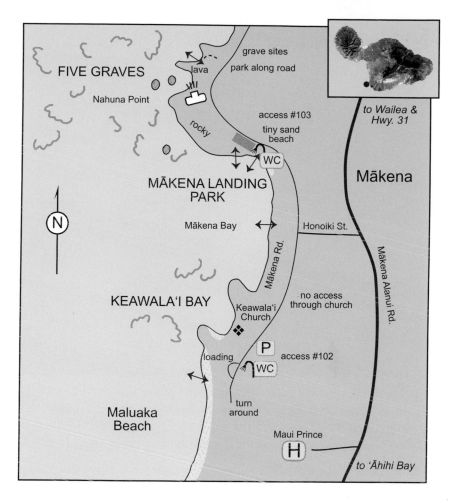

FIVE GRAVES

Nahuna Point

lava

grave sites
park along road

access #103

tiny sand
beach

to Wailea &
Hwy. 31

rocky

WC

MĀKENA LANDING
PARK

Mākena

Mākena Bay

Honoiki St.

Mākena Rd.

Mākena Alanui Rd.

N

KEAWALAʻI BAY

Keawalaʻi
Church

no access
through church

P

access #102

loading

WC

Maluaka
Beach

turn
around

Maui Prince

H

to ʻĀhihi Bay

GETTING THERE
Go south on Highway 31, turning right toward Wailea on Wailea Iki Drive, then left at The Shops at Wailea on Wailea Alanui Road (see area map, page 111). Watch for Mākena Road to your right just past the Mākena Surf condos. Just two tenths of a mile from the turnoff to Mākena Road, you'll reach the Five Graves area. There is a small amount of off street parking and a short well-marked "shoreline access" path zigzags towards the water, passing to the left of the graves and very close to the houses. This path angles toward a very narrow gap in the lava (on your right) where divers often enter. Entering from this "cove" is definitely not for beginners because the rocks are slippery and the surf unpredictable here. However, it does place you right in the middle of the best snorkeling. No facilities here, but people often are sunning on the lava shelf. For more parking, restrooms and shower, head south to nearby Mākena Landing Park.

Mākena Landing

For better parking and safer entry to Five Graves/Caves, but a longer swim, continue on Mākena Road to the Mākena Landing County Park (access #103), where you'll find a parking lot on the right with a shower and restrooms on the left near the sand (map, page 127).

Entry is best at the right side in the corner near the parking lot. There is a small, sandy beach offering easy access. Snorkel to the right and around the point as far as seems calm.

Another entry point is over rock from the middle of the parking lot. It's a bit trickier, but handy if the water's calm enough and you're careful to avoid slipping on the rocks. This gets you out closer to the point where you'll find the best snorkeling. There is also a neat little entry cove just ten feet beyond the parking lot, but it's marked "private property".

GETTING THERE
Go south on Highway 31, turning right toward Wailea on Wailea Iki Drive, then left on Wailea Alanui Road (see map, page 127). Watch for Mākena Road to your right just past the Mākena Surf condos. Continue on Mākena Road until you see the Mākena Landing County Park where you will see a parking lot with shower on the right and restrooms near the sand on the left.

Keawala'i Bay

Often called Church Bay, this small hidden bay offers fairly good snorkeling a short walk from a public parking area with shower and restrooms. Access to the bay is from the north end of Maluaka Bay, where Mākena Rd. ends. You'll need to snorkel to the right around the rocks to see the little bay behind the Keawala'i Church. All other access is blocked either by the church or by private homes. Entry is easy from the sandy, shallow beach as long as the swells aren't high. You will need to watch for rocks under the water—especially at low tide. The reef here is smaller than the one at the south end of the bay, but is typically uncrowded. A good choice on weekends.

South swell (most often in the summer) can hit this beach—especially in the afternoon. From the turn-around you'll be able to see both ends of Maluaka Beach and judge for yourself which has less swell. If you choose the south end, you'll need to double back and take the road just south of the Maui Prince Hotel (see page 137).

GETTING THERE   Heading south on Mākena Alanui Rd., take a right on Honoiki St.—the last turn before the Maui Prince Hotel. When Honoiki ends, turn left, then you'll pass the public parking lot with shower and restrooms on your left. Drop off passengers and gear at the turn around marked on our map (see page 127). Then double back to park. Don't try to find a shortcut through the church or private property since all access is well blocked.

Enter the water from the north end of the sandy beach and snorkel north (to the right) as far as conditions allow. This is a good place to watch for octopuses. Swim out a bit for deeper water where turtles hang out. Strong swimmers can go all the way to Mākena Bay, then hike back to parking.

Mel Malinowski

female psychedelic wrasse

129

Molokini Island

Molokini Island has become something of a legend—almost a mythical destination. It is certainly heavily advertised and promoted as a fantastic snorkeling spot. There's certainly some truth in this, but it's hard to separate the reality from the hype. How good is it, really?

Molokini is indeed a unique and interesting place, well worth visiting. A few decades ago, it had lots of coral and fish. Unfortunately, hurricane damage to the coral has left expanses of dead coral, and hence smaller fish counts. Still, you'll find a good variety of rather approachable fish, visibility almost always excellent and getting there takes you on a beautiful trip along the coast of Maui. This is also an excellent site for beginners and children. Most folks love their Molokini trip—especially when seas are fairly calm.

There are large numbers of excursions to choose from, so select your departure point, type of boat (if that's important to you), and a quality trip, if you care about the food, if you plan to dive or Snuba, or if you're a beginner and want good supervision and help. We seldom see as many fish or nearly as much coral as expected (the hype had given us, too, unrealistic expectations), but the variety of fish is excellent.The inside of the crater has little coral on the floor, but some large fish, eels, and the usual reef life.

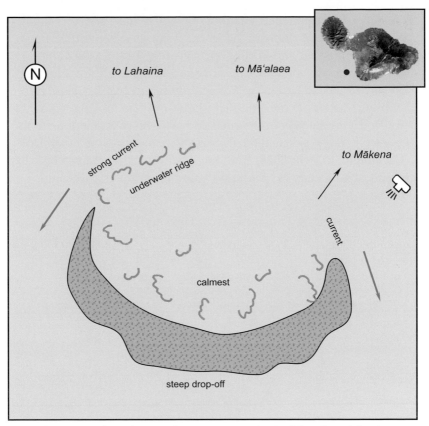

It can be somewhat choppy here even on the inside, since it's almost open ocean. Your excursion can offer life vests, noodles, or whatever it takes to make your experience easier. This is a perfect place to try the snorkels designed to keep choppy water out (even more useful later in the day).

Although there can be dozens of boats lined up inside the crater, it's a big place, and everyone seems to fit. Once you're in the water snorkeling, it doesn't seem crowded unless you stay near the boat. With more boats sharing the crater, we find they tend to restrict your available area—after all, the responsible excursions want to keep an eye on all their snorkelers. Even within the designated area, we have seen plenty of butterflyfish, bird wrasses, parrotfish, Moorish idols, tangs, triggerfish, and eels.

If your excursion happens to anchor at the edge of the crater, be very cautious before venturing past the edge of the crater. Strong currents are common at both outer edges of the island. Go there only with expert supervision no matter how well you swim.

For an unusual experience, tag along on a dive boat or take a smaller excursion to see the dramatic back side, with its sheer cliffs. The back sometimes has strong currents, so can be beyond the abilities of even the best swimmers. Carefully supervised drift dives are the best way to see the back side. For snorkeling, the back is similar to the front in terms of coral and fish (though you're looking mainly at a wall). It's completely uncrowded and even more dramatic with the sheer wall on one side and the deepest blue water on the other. Do NOT attempt to swim there from the inner crater! There can be killer currents at both ends of Molokini—good for a free trip to Tahiti.

We particularly enjoyed a chance to drift snorkel along the inner crater edge that's submerged (see map, page 131). This can only be done with a small boat on days when the current isn't too swift. Your captain will advise and supervise. We saw a manta ray and a white-tipped shark within minutes—quite a thrill. Then, on our very next trip we slid into the water from Maui Magic (in the center of the crater) and immediately swam with a ten-foot wide manta! Not a common sighting in the daytime, so perhaps we're awfully lucky. And the manta stuck around giving everyone a chance to see it.

132

Many excursions stop at a second site on the way back, so that you have a chance to see two sites. The reef off Five Graves is often the second site (see page 127) where you are almost certain to see plenty of turtles, thus the name Turtle Town. Other excursions stop at Coral Gardens (up near the Pali tunnel), which we prefer, for its better water clarity and pretty coral.

This is a good place for us to mention sea sickness medicines. Be sure to read our blue box "Motion Sickness" on page 21.

GETTING THERE

Numerous boat excursions leave early each morning from Mā'alaea Harbor, Kīhei small boat ramp, the Lahaina pier and even from hotel beaches. Some claim to be faster, but it makes little difference from our experience. You get out to sea and the race is on with most arriving at roughly the same time. Choose the departure location according to your convenience, since most of them leave so early (check in can be as early as 6 a.m.). Afternoon excursions are always cheaper, but you can count on the sea being choppier by then. Beginners will definitely prefer the morning excursions for calmer, easier snorkeling. If you choose afternoon, it's best to have a snorkel that keeps out the choppy water.

As more excursions are being added, some even leave super early and make three trips in one day. Some also depart from hotel beaches, which is convenient if it's your hotel. However, be warned that climbing a bouncing ladder from the beach can get pretty hairy when even small waves are washing through. If seas aren't calm we really don't recommend this very risky boarding for children, older folks, or pregnant women.

Parking is fairly easy and free at Mā'alaea, where you can find space near the pier or else near the aquarium—just a short hike (see map, page 103).

The Kīhei small boat ramp provides plenty of free parking, shade trees, picnic tables, restrooms and a shower (see map, page 101).

In Lahaina there are several lots near the harbor charging about $6 per day for parking. There aren't any good alternatives since roadside parking all over Lahaina is limited to a maximum of two hours (see map, page 88).

At all three departure points, you can drop passengers and gear near the boat, so one of you can check in while another parks. Some excursions ask that you check in at their office and pick up snorkeling gear before heading to the boat. Others distribute gear on the way to Molokini Island.

South Area

The rugged southernmost area of South Maui is definitely worth a visit, no matter where you are staying. This area extends from south of Mākena all the way around to south of Hāna, although you can't drive straight through. From Mākena you can only drive as far south as LaPérouse where the road ends. Beyond that you need at least 4WD. To connect with the south road to Hāna, you have to double all the way back up to Kahalui and then head south.

We highly recommend the southern beaches that you can reach from Wailea. The rest of the coast faces directly south and usually has rough water and strong currents. Snorkeling the far south is best done by boat access and even then, is not always possible. Your boat captain will make that decision.

There are no hotels after you pass the Maui Prince, but some excellent snorkeling when the water is both clear and calm, especially off the lava at 'Āhihi-Kīnaʻu. Black Sand and Little Beach also offer good snorkeling and are often calm, particularly in the mornings. 'Āhihi Cove is a gem when the water is clear, but can be surprisingly milky at times—for no obvious reason. When it's milky, the whole area through to La Pérouse is usually affected. Hiking across the lava gets you to dramatic and fragile sites, but is difficult and may not always be allowed.

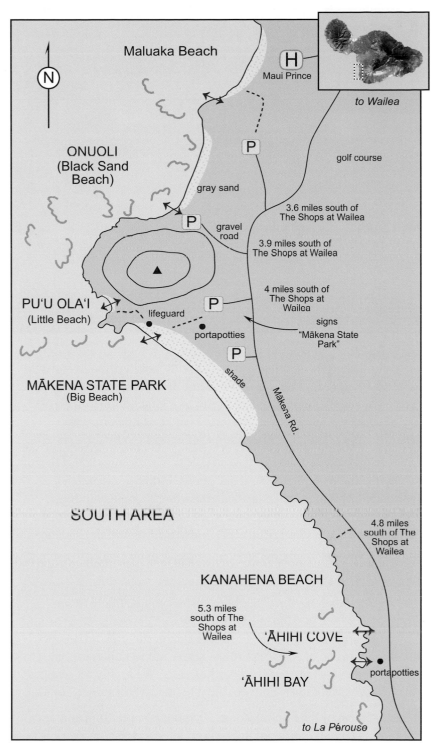

Maluaka Beach

N

H
Maui Prince

to Wailea

ONUOLI
(Black Sand
Beach)

golf course

P

gray sand

P

3.6 miles south of
The Shops at Wailea

gravel
road

3.9 miles south of
The Shops at Wailea

4 miles south of
The Shops at
Wailea

PU'U OLA'I
(Little Beach)

P

lifeguard

portapotties

signs
"Mākena State
Park"

P

shade

MĀKENA STATE PARK
(Big Beach)

Mākena Rd.

SOUTH AREA

4.8 miles
south of The
Shops at
Wailea

KANAHENA BEACH

5.3 miles
south of The
Shops at
Wailea

'ĀHIHI COVE

portapotties

'ĀHIHI BAY

to La Pérouse

135

Maluaka Beach

Maluaka Beach in front of the Maui Prince Hotel is an excellent all-around site. The south end of this lovely beach offers wonderful snorkeling and easy entry from the sand. It is serene, relatively uncrowned early in the day, and home to a large number of turtles. We have seen some Picasso triggerfish right near shore. This beautiful and relatively uncommon fish appears to be painted with water colors.

At the far south end of the beach a grassy hill has gorgeous views, picnic tables, shade, restrooms and showers. A great swimming, snorkeling or picnic spot. The view includes Molokini, Lāna'i, Kaho'olawe, Pu'u Ola'i (Red Hill) and West Maui in the distance.

Maluaka also tends to be fairly calm (especially before noon), so can be great for beginning snorkelers.

The further out you swim, the more turtles you're likely to see. This is where we saw the largest turtle we've encountered in Maui. Mornings are best, since the wind and swells can pick up around noon. This is one of Maui's prettiest spots and remains surprisingly uncrowded except on weekends or holidays. We highly recommend this beach as well as the conveniently-located Maui Prince Hotel.

The north end of the beach also offers modest snorkeling and fair swimming (if you can avoid the basketball-sized rocks). Entry is

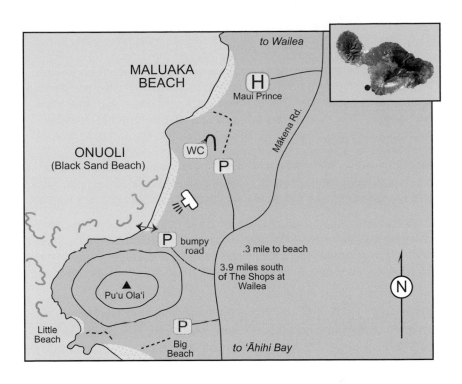

MALUAKA
BEACH

to Wailea

(H)
Maui Prince

ONUOLI
(Black Sand Beach)

WC

P

Mākena Rd.

P bumpy
road

.3 mile to beach

3.9 miles south
of The Shops at
Wailea

(N)

▲
Pu'u Ola'i

P

Little
Beach

Big
Beach

to 'Āhihi Bay

Picasso (lagoon) triggerfish

easiest right near the point where you'll find a narrow sandy and
gradual "path" through the water. This helps because the beach is
very shallow and rocky nearby. Out around the point we have seen
healthy coral, two turtles, two octopuses, a whitemouth moray, and
many of the usual reef fish, but not huge numbers of fish. Public
parking is available nearby as well as restrooms and a shower with
the highest water pressure we've ever encountered—like rinsing off
in a firehose!

137

GETTING THERE   Going south on Highway 31, turn

right toward Wailea on Wailea Iki Drive (see map, page 137). High-way 31 dead ends here. At The Shops at Wailea turn left on Wailea Alanui Road. Note your mileage at this point. In 3.6 miles you'll see a small road on your right that doubles back and has a sign that says "dead end". This road is very easy to miss if you forget to note the mileage (see map, page 111). There is a golf path on the far side of the little road, so you'll know it's the right one. Take this a short few blocks to the small parking lot holding about twenty cars in each of two lots. There's an easy path to the beach—about 100 yards. You'll see restrooms and picnic tables on your left. To the right is a shower.

Snorkel along the reef on the left, which is quite extensive. In calm weather, you can snorkel directly over the reef with plenty of clearance for an excellent close-up view of the coral and fish. In calm weather with bright sun, this reef is delightful. Stay outside the reef's edge when swell gets higher, especially at low tide.

An access to the north end of the beach is from Mākena Road. On your left you'll find a public parking lot with about fifty spaces with restrooms and shower about 200 yards before you get to the north end of the beach. Passengers can be dropped off in the "loading zone" even closer to the sandy entry spot. There is no other access through the church property or the private homes. From this end of the beach you can snorkel to the right and around the point to an area in front of the church opposite the public parking lot (see map, page 137). We prefer the south end of Maluaka when conditions are good there, but sometimes we choose whichever end is calmer.

Onuoli Beach (Black Sand Beach)

This beach is uncrowded, compared with the rest of Mākena State Park because it doesn't offer particularly good swimming or surfing. The beach is quite shallow with coral near the shore making it more challenging at low tide. Snorkeling is excellent near the cliffs, but not spectacular in the shallow areas near shore. If you don't see turtles, just continue out to the deeper water (about twenty feet deep). When seas are calm, a strong swimmer can snorkel all the way around the red cliffs to Puʻu Olaʻi. This site offers some protection from summer south swell that can hit Big Beach quite hard.

Black Sand Beach is better for snorkeling than swimming since the whole beach contains coral near shore. There aren't terrific numbers of fish. Still, there's an excellent variety of some of the prettiest fish with turtles almost a sure sighting. No facilities are available here, other than a gravel parking lot right near the shore. When waves do arrive at Black Sand Beach, it's best to snorkel elsewhere because you don't want to get caught between coral and waves.

GETTING THERE

Going south on Highway 31, take Wailea Iki to the right until you see The Shops at Wailea. Here, take Wailea Alanui Road south (noting the mileage at this corner). At 3.9 miles from this corner you'll see a dirt road toward Red Hill (see site map, page 137). This .3-mile road winds back to Black Sand Beach (really sort of gray as you can see from the picture), where you can park near the sea. When very calm, this is a good site for beginners. More experienced snorkelers will enjoy heading around the hill to the left (south) as far as Pu'u Ola'i Beach as well as out to sea. Be alert for the coral that lies all along the shore and don't snorkel here when the surf is up or the tide is too low. Early morning is definitely best since you need to swim over a band of coral that is within a couple of feet of the surface.

Pu'u Ola'i (Little Beach)

Pu'u Ola'i is usually called Little Beach. From the parking lot at Oneloa, also called Big Beach, where the sign says "Mākena State Park", walk straight down the shady, flat path to the long, sandy beach with some facilities (picnic tables, portable toilets, no shower) and a lifeguard at times.

This is a very popular swimming, sunbathing, and surfing spot with plenty of sand and some shade. Just beyond the lifeguard station at the far right is a path leading up the hill to Pu'u Ola'i, which is a traditional nude beach. It also happens to be an excellent snorkeling and swimming spot when calm.

From the beach at Pu'i Ola'i, snorkel to the right as far as it is calm enough—or even straight out to sea. There are lots of little canyons, coves, good coral, large and numerous turtles, and plenty of fish variety (although not huge numbers of fish). The snorkeling is definitely worth the hike. When the sea is calm, you can snorkel all the way around either point, with good snorkeling the entire way.

Note: To avoid confusion, remember there are other Mākena and Oneloa beaches on Maui, thus the popularity of the names Big and

140

Little. Onuoli Beach to the north of Puʻu Olaʻi is also called Black Sand Beach and also has a sign that says Mākena State Park.

Although our picture is too small for you to notice fine details, none of the folks in the picture are bothering with bathing suits. If that makes you uncomfortable, party elsewhere. If you want to snorkel here in a bathing suit anyway, no one is likely to mind.

GETTING THERE
Going south on Highway 31, turn right on Wailea Iki Drive toward The Shops at Wailea, then left on Wailea Alanui Road and continue south. The Big Beach turnoff is 4 miles south of this point (see map, page 135). This is the old parking lot, but provides the best access to the north end of the beach and to Little Beach. A new and larger lot has been built two tenths of a mile to the south.

At the beach side of the parking lot is a path marked with a sign that says "Mākena State Park". Follow the path 180 yards to the beach, then continue across the sand to the right past the lifeguard station until you see a narrow path over the small hill (about fifty feet high). Walk 240 yards to Puʻu Olaʻi (Little Beach). It's a fairly easy path, but not flat, and requires some minor climbing over the edge of the hill.

Maui skimboarder

Oneloa Beach (Big Beach)

This popular beach, usually called Big Beach, is best for swimming, sunning, picnics and socializing. It often has a fair surf, and is popular for body surfing and boogie boarding. At times (especially with southern swell), it can be too rough for safety.

Snorkeling is best around the point between Big and Little Beaches, and is possible only when conditions are calm enough. It is often possible to snorkel all the way to Puʻu Olaʻi from the northern end near the lifeguard station at Big Beach. Mornings are almost always better here for snorkelers because the waves usually pick up in the early afternoon.

If you want to snorkel, be sure to park in the lot at the far north since this is indeed one BIG Beach. You'll find plenty of wide sandy beach, picnic tables, portable toilets, but no showers. Beginners will find the hike to Puʻu Olaʻi much easier than the long snorkel even on a calm day. Strong swimmers (preferably with wetsuits) can snorkel all the way from Big Beach to Black Sand Beach.

GETTING THERE
Going south on Highway 31, turn right on Wailea Iki Drive. At The Shops at Wailea, note the mileage, turn left on Wailea Alanui Road and continue south for four miles. This is the old parking lot and is the one closest to the snorkeling. There is a larger parking lot at the next exit to the south. On the beach side of the parking lot, you will see a wide path marked "Mākena State Park" and it takes you down a shady path directly to the beach, about 180 yards (see area map, page 135).

Mel Malinowski

female bird wrasse

Mel Malinowski

male bird wrasse

143

Kanahena Beach

This beautiful hidden beach offers a pleasant, unusual picnic spot (particularly in the summer or fall) after you snorkel ʻĀhihi Cove, which has no sand. Kanahena is completely hidden from view, although right next to Mākena Road, reached from a short path squeezed between two stylish oceanfront homes. The sand at this tiny beach is powdery soft and white—with quite a bit more sand in the summer and fall. Ringed by palms, bougainvillaea, high stone walls and a view of Molokini and Kahoʻolawe, it offers a secluded spot to relax, wade, and enjoy the beauty. If you try it, you may have the beach to yourselves! Modest snorkeling is possible, but only when there is high tide and no swell at all, due to lots of sharp ʻaʻa rocks. Good sheltered wading for kids, but too shallow and rocky for an easy swim. No facilities.

GETTING THERE   Going south on Mākena Road, about half a mile south of Big Beach, watch for a high stone wall on the ocean side of the road (see area map, page 135). This small beach is completely hidden from the road. There is a five-foot wide gap in the wall for beach access (blue "shoreline access" sign) just south of house #6900. Across the street (mauka) you will see house #6925 with a chain link fence. Take the narrow twenty-foot path to the sand. Parking is very limited.

Snorkel Gear Rentals

Should you rent, or buy? It really depends on your level of experience, and whether you expect to continue to snorkel regularly. If you're new to snorkeling, renting for a few times is a good idea, so you can try out various types of gear.

Snorkel gear rental is very competitive on Maui with plenty of shops scattered around the island. Snorkel Bob's, Boss Frog and Maui Dive Shop have the most outlets. They often advertise mask, snorkel, fins, etc. all for the low, low price of $9.95 per week, or $1 a day and such. This is just to get you in the shop, where they can sell you up to better quality, more expensive gear. We'd guess few people actually rent the bottom of the line stuff. Those who do probably later wish they hadn't. You're much more likely to pick the "dry" snorkel, comfortable mask, and prescription lenses. Expect to pay at least $30-40 for a week.

If you're really going to take up snorkeling or stay more than a week, and you have snorkeled before, perhaps you'd be better off buying your gear. You might want to check out more than one shop since most carry a limited selection. Snorkel Bob's even sells kid's packages with the agreement that you can trade it all in for partial credit when junior outgrows his. The larger size will run you half off if you trade in last year's gear.

The basic rubber fins are OK at first, but people tend to develop definite preferences over time. Leg strength will influence your choice and fit is always personal. If you do buy, make sure you can snorkel for at least an hour without getting blisters. Don't you just hate it when you buy a pair of $100 fins and then find they hurt your feet?

If you discover that your rental gear isn't fitting properly, take it back for an exchange or upgrade.

If you are near-sighted, a corrective mask is a must. Corrective lenses are available for anothing up to about 10 diopters. If you have unusual problems, such as astigmatism or quite unequal corrections, you'd have to have a special mask made in advance. Far-sighted folks benefit from a bifocal mask, which enables better up-close fish viewing, as well as watch or dive gauge reading. These cannot be rented.

'Āhihi Cove

One of our Maui favorites, this gem is a beautiful tiny cove with fairly clear water and lots to see—even a large eel close to shore to awe the little kids. Entry is a bit slippery from the old concrete boat ramp at the far right, so sit down and work your way in very carefully, especially if you encounter any swell.

The cove itself is quite calm and shallow (five to fifteen feet deep) and the reef extends far out. This bay has a wonderful variety within a small space, so it is well worth the drive even if you're staying in the north. Another must see!

Beginners can have a great time close to shore where there are plenty of large and varied fish. More advanced snorkelers can venture out beyond into the larger bay. This is actually a tiny cove within a large, protected area. It has too much coral and sharp rock to be a good swimming spot, but snorkelers can see where they're going. Snorkel any direction. It's all fascinating, but has no facilities and only a tiny, rocky beach.

We have seen huge parrotfish, all sorts of butterflyfish and tangs, Moorish idols, triggerfish, wrasses and much more, like a large aquarium, but from the inside. Out further to the left we have seen octopus and beautiful coral. If it's calm enough, swim way out to the left. The right side is good too. Don't miss this bay! Beginners

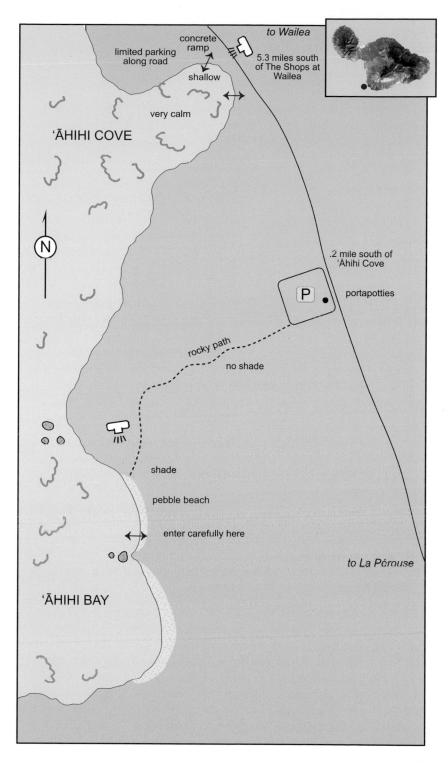

to Wailea

concrete ramp

limited parking along road

5.3 miles south of The Shops at Wailea

shallow

very calm

'ĀHIHI COVE

N

.2 mile south of 'Āhihi Cove

P

portapotties

rocky path

no shade

shade

pebble beach

enter carefully here

to La Pérouse

'ĀHIHI BAY

147

should practice elsewhere first until competent enough to avoid kicking the fragile reef. There are no sandy areas for beginners to stop and stand. Entry can be tricky when south swell is high, since the entry area is shallow and rocky.

At times the water all along this area can be milky-looking making for terrible visibility (especially near shore), but with even ten-foot visibility, it's worth a snorkel.

As more snorkelers arrive at tiny 'Āhihi Cove, they will inevitably take a toll on the coral. We strongly recommend that beginners go to the much larger area just to the south. Go to 'Āhihi Cove only if you can keep from touching any of the coral and forego sunscreen. Remember that this site will be made off limits if it gets treated badly. The cove is very small and very fragile compared to the larger areas of 'Āhihi-Kīna'u Reserve.

GETTING THERE

Going south on Highway 31, take the Wailea Iki Drive turnoff to the right toward the hotels (see area map, page 135). Then at The Shops at Wailea, turn left on Wailea Alanui Road. Note the mileage at this intersection in order to determine the location of several of these beaches. 'Āhihi Cove is 5.3 miles south of this intersection. The road will continue south eventually crossing bare lava, narrow but still an adequate road.

First you'll see walls surrounding some lovely multimillion dollar homes. Then at 'Āhihi Cove, you'll see the cove on your right as the road narrows to one lane and curves left, skirting the tiny cove. You'll also see some houses and trees here (see site map, page 147). Park along the road wherever there is a legal spot. Parking is no longer allowed on the side of the road in most of this area, but there are a few spaces just before the cove and even more just past the cove. If parking at the cove fills (which it usually does quite early), there is a dirt parking lot just two tenths of a mile further south. You'll find a couple of portapotties there and sometimes a table with literature about the 'Āhihi-Kīna'u Reserve.

Enter the water on the far right (north) corner of the cove, only ten feet from the road. The old concrete ramp provides a little slide into the water. The beach itself is rocky rather than sandy and quite small. Just so you're sure this is the right place—you'll see stone walls and a telephone pole marked T5 just before the cove. Avoid when waves hit the shore because this inner cove is all very shallow and filled with sharp coral. Depending on the exact direction of a bit of swell, it can sometimes be easier to enter near the south corner of the bay, but watch for sharp lava and black sea urchins.

148

spotted surgeonfish

'Āhihi Bay

You'll find a gravel parking lot exactly .2 of a mile south of 'Āhihi Cove. This is an extensive and excellent spot for experienced snorkelers. It's suited to beginners when calm or swimmers if they can avoid the rocks and coral.

There's ample space in the dirt parking lot and a couple of portable toilets on the far left. You must hike down a somewhat rocky path with little shade until you reach the beach. Shoes are a must here.

Snorkeling is uncrowded and excellent with great views of Haleakala in the background and Molokini Island out to sea. Be sure to lift your head out of the water now and then to enjoy the fabulous views towards shore. You'll want to try this one more than once because it offers such a large area to explore.

We have seen turtles, eels, scrawled filefish, sailfin tangs, frogfish and a huge school of Heller's barracuda (just after entering the water). Come early in the day for the calmest conditions. You'll want to snorkel for a long time, so wear a wetsuit if you have one. We highly recommend this whole snorkeling area if you are even moderately experienced and conditions are calm. On occasion this area gets very murky with a milky look. When this happens, you're better off in a shallower area where everything is closer to your face.

GETTING THERE

Go two tenths of a mile past 'Āhihi Cove and turn right, parking in this open area (see map, page 147). The path starts straight toward the water and angles to the left until it reaches the rocky beach (about 200 yards of relatively easy path— compared to the 'a'a lava on both sides). At the beach, continue another 100 yards south (to your left) across the gravel beach to just before the next little point where entry is easier over a bit of sand.

There's a nice shady spot to leave your stuff and you'll find the entry easier than it appears from a distance. Once out in the bay, snorkel to the right near shore as well as further out to see the variety. Our favorite spot is off the point about halfway to 'Āhihi Cove. Entry is quite easy but you should make sure to return to the same spot. If you'd like a one-way snorkel, swim all the way into 'Āhihi Cove and hike back to your car. Of course, this one-way snorkel works best if you wear booties or carry plastic flip-flops along as you snorkel.

green sea turtle being cleaned by yellow tangs

'Āhihi-Kīna'u Reserve

'Āhihi-Kīna'u Natural Area Reserve is a large cape created by the last major lava flow on Maui in 1790. Previously this was a long sandy beach, but lava built out toward the sea resulting in this starkly beautiful and rugged terrain. Hawai'ians are attempting to protect this fragile beauty that includes archeological ruins and a fairly young reef. Parking has been eliminated between 'Āhihi Bay and La Pérouse and trails have been purposely obscured in an effort to discourage visitors. Nothing may be disturbed or taken from this area—including shells and lava.

Since the two main trails are difficult to find, far from parking, and VERY rough, we recommend them only for sturdy hikers who take great care to leave the environment undisturbed. This means hiking shoes, hats, plenty of water and no sunscreen. Take a good look at the 'a'a lava and imagine how much fun you'd have getting lost out here and trying to hike cross country! These trails are barely marked to discourage tourists. In the future any of them might be closed.

For most people, 'Āhihi Bay is a far better choice than Fish Pond. The bay has a large mature reef waiting to be explored. Aquarium can be reached from La Pérouse Bay without having to hike over the lava. You'll find both paths on our map, but neither is easy or particularly safe. These paths are definitely not for children or older folks, who would not appreciate falling on the sharp 'a'a lava.

Parking has been removed or blocked off by boulders to discourage people from using the fragile areas where paths lead to Fish Pond and Aquarium. Other connecting paths are nearly impossible to follow and dangerous, so there's no way tourists should consider them. This rugged coast is best explored by kayak with a guide.

Fish Pond

This trail across sharp 'a'a lava is VERY difficult to spot and requires a half-hour hike. We'll tell you where it is, but don't try this one with young children or older people. Also, you'll first have to hike half a mile from parking, must wear sturdy shoes, carry water and cover up to avoid using sunscreen in the tiny cove. Hawai'ians are trying hard to preserve this fragile area, so please keep in mind that you are hiking through important archeological ground.

152

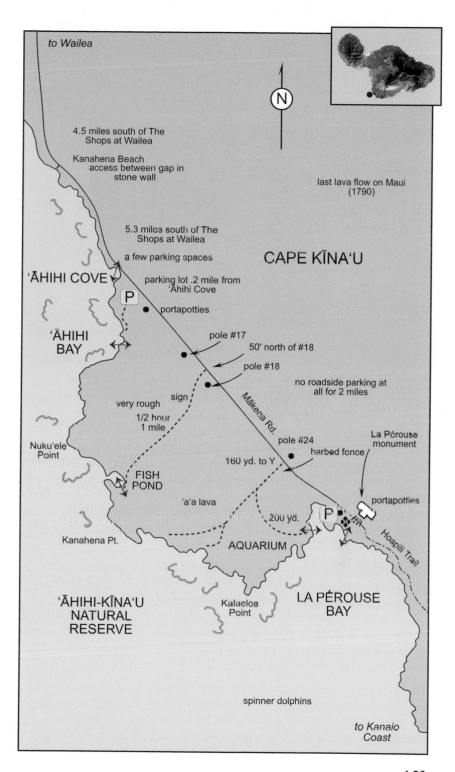

to Wailea

N

4.5 miles south of The
Shops at Wailea

Kanahena Beach
access between gap in
stone wall

last lava flow on Maui
(1790)

5.3 miles south of The
Shops at Wailea

a few parking spaces

CAPE KĪNAʻU

'ĀHIHI COVE

parking lot .2 mile from
'Āhihi Cove

P

portapotties

'ĀHIHI
BAY

pole #17

50' north of #18

pole #18

no roadside parking at
all for 2 miles

sign

very rough

Mākena Rd.

1/2 hour
1 mile

Nukuʻele
Point

pole #24

La Pérouse
monument

160 yd. to Y

barbed fence

FISH
POND

'a'a lava

P

portapotties

200 yd.

Kanahena Pt.

AQUARIUM

Hoapili Trail

'ĀHIHI-KĪNAʻU
NATURAL
RESERVE

Kalaeloa
Point

LA PÉROUSE
BAY

spinner dolphins

to Kanaio
Coast

The snorkeling area is tiny, but excellent with lots of small colorful fish. When seas are unusually calm, you can snorkel out beyond the cove in either direction. These days more kayakers are arriving, so you may not have the little cove to yourselves. No faciletes or shade here. The nearest portapotties are at 'Āhihi Bay.

GETTING THERE
Driving south on Highway 31, turn right on Wailea Iki Dr. toward The Shops at Wailea (see map, page 147). Note your mileage at the shops, head left on Wailea Alanui Rd. Continue past 'Āhihi Bay, which is 5.3 miles from this corner. Less than a mile past the bay, you'll see telephone pole #17. Watch for the next telephone pole, which should be #18, but isn't marked (see map, page 153). The unmarked trail to the water starts fifty feet north of this pole. Parking is no longer available anywhere between 'Āhihi and La Pérouse, making this site even more challenging by land. The trail is unmarked except for some splashes of white paint—none of them visible from the start of the trail.

The first part of the trail has been disguised and definitely doesn't look promising, but gets easier soon. You'll know you're on the trail when you see the sign "'Āhihi-Kīna'u Reserve" about twenty yards in from the road. Follow this trail very carefully all the way to the water, where entry is quite easy from a pebble beach. Watch the trail as you go to ensure you won't get lost on your return. No cell coverage in this southern area!

There is a connecting trail of sorts leading south to the next trail we mention, however, it is not well marked and VERY difficult to follow. It's easy to get lost here and you'll want to be back well before dark. Getting lost on this sharp 'a'a lava in the full sun is not fun!

154

Aquarium

Heading south toward La Pérouse, there is an easier trail over the lava field that will take you to Aquarium (a protected bay just north of La Pérouse Bay). This trail is considerably easier than the one to Fish Pond, however, you still need to treat the area with great respect. Aquarium can be reached just as well by swimming from the parking area at La Pérouse itself. The main advantage of the trail is that the entry can be quite calm compared to the beach at La Pérouse. This whole area is within the reserve, so no collecting of any sort, and be extremely careful to not disturb anything on land or in the sea. Do not even use sunscreen. Bring your own shade and water. Hiking shoes are helpful. No facilities except portapotties back in the La Pérouse parking area. No cell coverage.

At times this whole area gets very milky looking, making snorkeling quite disappointing. When it's clear though, it's delightful. If you come on a calm day, experienced snorkelers can wander beyond this inner bay as far as water conditions allow. Water clarity often improves as you swim away (to the right) from the sandy beaches.

GETTING THERE   Driving south on Highway 31, turn right on Wailea Iki Dr. toward The Shops at Wailea, then head south on Wailea Alanui Rd. Continue to the end the road, where a dirt 4WD road starts at La Pérouse. Either park in the lot on your right or double back to the roadside parking just south of the "no parking" signs, where there is room for about five cars along the mauka side of the road (see site map, page 153).

The trail starts at the north end of the barbed wire fence. The first part of the trail that follows the fence toward the ocean is sandy and fairly easy. At the end of the fence, you'll see the bay, but will need to hike over black lava with no shade and certainly no facilities. We prefer swimming from La Pérouse, unless the choppy water makes entry difficult. In that case, hike to the bay where the entry is calm. Swim out around the point to the right when very calm seas permit.

La Pérouse Bay

When the English explorer Captain Cook made the first European contact with Hawai'i in 1778, he described and mapped a large bay stretching from the great cinder cone Pu'u Ola'i in the north, to Cape Hanamanoia in the south. Called 'Āhihi Bay, it had a magnificent long sandy beach.

Another English sailor, Vancouver, arrived here in 1792 and described a very different coastline. In 1790, the last great lava flow on Maui had formed Cape Kīna'u, projecting more than a mile out and two miles wide right in the middle of 'Āhihi Bay! Hawai'ian fast-lane geology at work!

At La Pérouse Bay, even slight surf or swell can make entry tricky because it's rocky and slippery. Try it only in the morning when completely calm. This site is rarely calm enough for beginners, but it offers good snorkeling for those who like to explore. La Pérouse can be very murky (almost milky)—especially near the shore, so check local conditions before trying this spot. Less experienced snorkelers are much better off at 'Āhihi Bay. First-time snorkelers should stick with shallow, sandy beaches further north.

GETTING THERE

Driving south on Highway 31, take the Wailea Iki turnoff right towards the big resorts (see area map, page 135). Then turn left on Wailea Alanui Rd. Continue south as the road gets smaller and crosses bare lava. Pass the little bay and pass the 'Āhihi-Kīna'u sign (see site map, page 153). Seven miles south of the shops, you'll come to the end of the road, where you'll find a dirt parking area. On your left will be the La Pérouse Memorial monument. Just past the monument on the right is the beach with parking and some portapotties. A dirt 4WD road continues south in case you want to walk down to the sandy beach.

You might want to try La Pérouse from one of the excursions, which can take you out where the water tends to be more clear. It is often milky-looking near the beach.

Kanaio Coast

The dramatic and beautiful black lava Kanaio Coast is accessible only by boat or rugged 4WD and some rock climbing. When south swell isn't too high, there's exciting snorkeling available in the many small coves formed when Maui's most recent lava flow produced these rugged cliffs. You could hardly find a prettier area to swim or snorkel—especially where there are black basalt columns or large lava arches in the background. Excursions such as Blue Water Rafting with their zodiac-style rafts depart from the Kīhei boat ramp when conditions permit. A complete lack of sand in this area helps keep the water quite clear. Keep the south in mind when far-away winter storms bring huge surf up north.

GETTING THERE   Since Highway 31 (Pi'ilani Highway) in Wailea doesn't connect with the southern section of 31, there's no way to drive to this section of the south coast. Even if the highway is ever connected, the land here is rugged enough that you couldn't easily reach the sea.

Try checking with Blue Waters Rafting for their zodiac-style rafts that can zip down here in no time. Keep in mind that conditions are frequently rough here due to the south exposure, wind, and lack of any protecting reef. In fact, it's often too rough for the boats—6-8 foot swells are common and currents can be very strong at any time. Don't try the south on your own—even if you're experienced.

East Area

We continue describing sites in a counterclockwise direction, which takes us along the far south of Maui over to Hāna.

At this point the only way through to the south is to double back to the Haleakala Highway and take Highway 37 down to the eastern section of Highway 31. This trip eventually follows the rugged south shore on up to the Hāna area in the east. Very few tourists (or anyone else for that matter) take this road, but it's entirely adequate unless closed due to earthquake or flood. As the road approaches Hāna it gets rough on and off, but not with deep ruts—just very bouncy. We like going to Hāna one way and returning the other. The scenery in the south is entirely different from the famed road to Hāna, but equally beautiful. Gas up first and take food and water.

East Maui offers a wonderful day trip, but it's a LONG day. The Hāna Highway takes at least two hours each way from Kahului, and longer when you stop a bit to enjoy the gorgeous views and waterfalls. It's an extremely slow road with countless twists and turns and very little passing, so prepare to take your time and soak in the sight of jungle greenery here on the wet side of Maui.

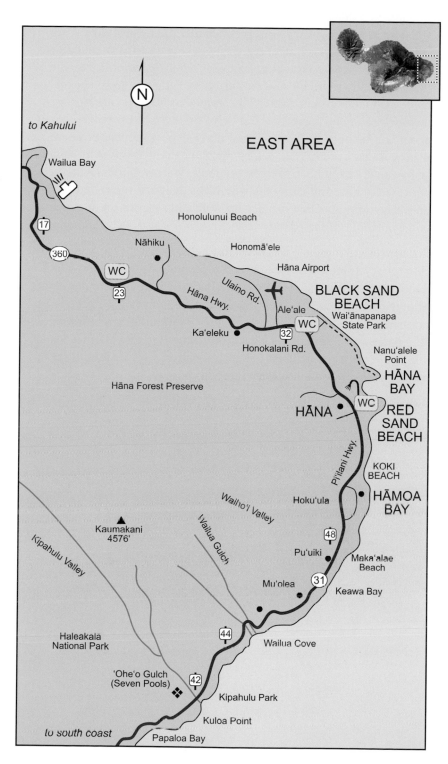

EAST AREA

to Kahului

Wailua Bay

Honolulunui Beach

17

Nāhiku

Honomā'ele

360

WC

Hāna Airport

23

Ulaino Rd.

BLACK SAND
BEACH

Hāna Hwy.

Ale'ale

Wai'ānapanapa
State Park

Ka'eleku

WC

32

Honokalani Rd.

Nanu'alele
Point

Hāna Forest Preserve

HĀNA
BAY

HĀNA

WC

RED
SAND
BEACH

Pi'ilani Hwy.

KOKI
BEACH

Wailo'i Valley

Hoku'ula

HĀMOA
BAY

Kaumakani
4576'

Wailua Gulch

48

Kipahulu Valley

Pu'uiki

Maka'alae
Beach

Mu'olea

31

Keawa Bay

Haleakala
National Park

44

Wailua Cove

'Ohe'o Gulch
(Seven Pools)

42

Kipahulu Park

Kuloa Point

to south coast

Papaloa Bay

Hāna itself is a tiny town with great charm and beautiful beaches. While you can snorkel here, the west coast is usually much calmer and more reliable, so travel to Hāna for other reasons. The Seven Pools (actually more like twelve) are now called by their Hawaiʻian name of ʻOheʻo Gulch. Waterfalls abound at ʻOheʻo Gulch, but so do tourists, so don't expect a fast drive on this narrow road (usually about half an hour from Hāna) and don't expect seclusion. There are plenty of other pretty pools and waterfalls along the road to Hāna and you may even have them to yourself. Wailua Gulch is another nice area to hike and enjoy the waterfalls. Keep in mind that Maui does have droughts that can dry up waterfalls—even on this green windward side of the island.

For beaches that are always beautiful and sometimes calm enough to snorkel, try Hāna Bay, Hāmoa Beach, Red Sand Beach, and Black Sand Beach in Waiʻānapanapa State Park. Although there are plenty of other lovely beaches, most catch the swells from the prevailing northeast trades and are seldom safe for swimming or snorkeling. When unsure of conditions, check out Hāna Bay and Hāmoa Beach which are often the calmest. We also mention Koki, but only for its beauty. Koki Beach is the least likely to be safe.

Dive Boats

PADI and NAUI attempt to regulate the diving industry with strict rules, since there are serious risks involved. No one is allowed to dive without certification (backed up by a C Card). Anyone who wants to dive without proper training is certainly a fool, and the shops who will take such rash people out are equally foolish.

We have seen excursions all over the world offering to take people down without proof of certification. This is not the mark of the highest level of safety consciousness. Keep in mind that other advice and services from such operators may be similarly casual. Always take extra care with any rental equipment.

When their business is slow, some take divers (or snorkelers) to sites they can't handle. On the better snorkeling excursions, they keep a close eye on all their charges, so it's like having a lifeguard along.

Tagging along with a dive boat, you may find yourself on the surface as a snorkeler in much rougher conditions than the divers sixty feet beneath you. You'll need to rely on a buddy since the crew is usually more focused on the divers. It's a good idea to ask in advance whether good snorkeling is possible at the particular dive site they are planning for that day.

Most dive operators run safe, well-organized excursions, and welcome snorkelers on appropriate dives. Don't be afraid to ask up front what their policies and attitudes are.

ornate wrasse

161

Hāmoa Bay

As you continue on around Maui counterclockwise (not that the road connects well—you may in fact prefer coming around the other way), the next good snorkeling is in the Hāna area. Northeast swells often keep the waves and currents strong. But when swells do calm down, there is some excellent snorkeling here.

Hāmoa Bay has one of Maui's most beautiful white-sand beaches in a lush location. Snorkeling is definitely meager and you need to swim out a ways to see some fish. Still, the beach is beautiful, and well worth a visit—best perhaps for a cool swim after the long drive to Hāna.

If you decide to snorkel, head out along the left side to the protecting reef offshore. If waves and current permit, make a circle and continue on to the right side. Entry is very easy from the sand as long as the water is calm. Although we haven't seen much coral, we do see sailfin tangs, rectangular triggerfish and other interesting fish. Not a bad spot for learning how to snorkel, but only when it is calm.

162

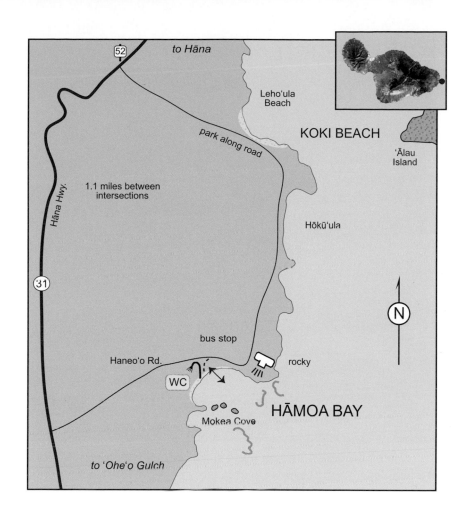

GETTING THERE   From the town of Hāna, head south on the Hāna Highway for one mile. This is where Haneo'o Road curves off to the left looping to the water before returning to the highway. The quickest way is to take the second Haneo'o exit to the left. At four tenths of a mile from the highway, you'll see a bus stop on your right. Parking close is the challenge. It's unlikely you'll find anything right by the stairs, which start just west of the bus stop. No parking is allowed on the ocean side of the road. Next to the bus stop there's a 75-yard concrete path with 21 steps down to the beach, where you'll find restrooms, showers and some food. Enter the water right at the end of the stairs for either swimming or snorkeling in this gorgeous spot. Don't miss it.

163

Koki Beach

Just around the corner driving north from Hāmoa Beach you'll find this dramatic beach. There's a picnic table in the shade where you can enjoy a picnic and the view of Alau Island with its clump of palms on the top. This is really two beaches with another to the right.

When the sky is clear, you can see Mauna Kea and sometimes Mauna Loa on the Big Island. You'll also see the large sign indicating Koki is a dangerous beach (pictured on page 165). Take its advice seriously. While it's possible to find the water calm here, you'd have to be very lucky.

Good for boogie boarding at times if you're a very good swimmer and have friends who are qualified to rescue you. Otherwise, just enjoy the view and picnicking. No facilities except for portapotties at the southern end of the two adjoining beaches.

GETTING THERE
From Hāmoa Beach, continue to the north and you'll see Koki. There's a sign and the beach has parking right beside the road.

From Hāna, go south on Highway 31 to the north end of Haneo'o Road (see site map, page 163). Turn left here and you can't miss the two Koki Beaches.

Mel Malinowski

peacock flounder

Red Sand Beach

When Hāna has calm water, this beach is a special treat. The only drawback is a relatively smooth access path that looks safe, but is actually slippery and quite dangerous. Wear shoes with some tread (not smooth-soled flip-flops) and walk carefully to avoid slipping and sliding right over the edge. This mixture of dry powder and red lava cinder particles can work like little ball bearings. Because the path is narrow and on a steep sidehill, if you slide over the edge, you may find yourself on an unstoppable sleigh ride to the edge of a small cliff, and down onto the rocks, and serious injury. Ouch!

The trail is popular, nevertheless, and many folks negotiate it just fine, using a little care. We like the place so much, we walk it with care. Another option is by kayak with an experienced guide. You'll find them back at Hāna Bay just around the far point.

The trail just south of Hāna School takes you to this well-hidden beach, popular with snorkelers and nudists. Rounding the corner, the view is spectacular. You look out upon the remains of an unusual cinder cone with a natural breakwater protecting a shallow pond. You can snorkel in the shallow water, but won't see much. The real action is through the channel outside the natural breakwater, where we have seen lots of bandit angelfish, schools of Moorish idols, and even a solitary reef squid (seldom seen in Maui).

166

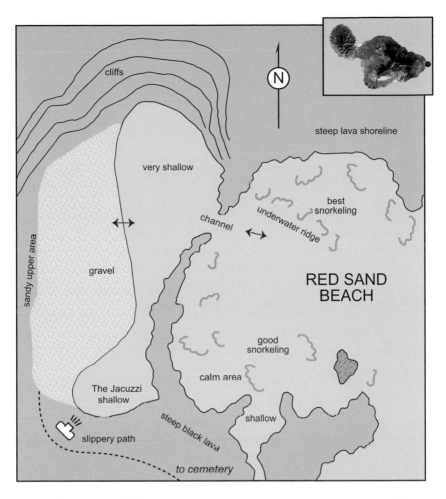

cliffs

N

steep lava shoreline

very shallow

channel

underwater ridge

best snorkeling

sandy upper area

gravel

RED SAND BEACH

good snorkeling

The Jacuzzi shallow

calm area

steep black lava

shallow

slippery path

to cemetery

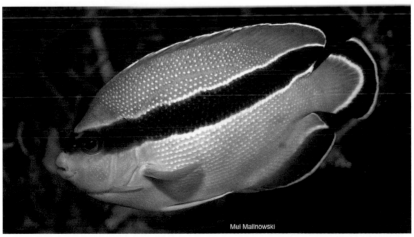

Mel Malinowski

bandit angelfish

167

First, a word about a channel like this one. When seas are rough or when the tide is going out, a channel funnels the water making it much swifter! You must test first before exiting the channel. There's no lifeguard to rescue you if it's impossible to swim back against the tide. Even the best swimmer could have trouble here when tide heads out or when waves are pouring over the breakwater and that water has to get out somehow. It's helpful to check on the tides and swell conditions before heading for Red Sand Beach. Exercise caution!

This tiny cove is unusual, interesting, secluded, and one of our favorites. It isn't the best place for beginners or those who avoid choppy water, but experienced snorkelers will love swimming out the channel where there's lots to see in ten to twenty-foot deep water. This outer area is somewhat protected by points further out. Keep within this outer protected bay unless the water is unusually calm and be sure to check out the view back toward the crater. No facilities. Swimsuits appear to be optional.

GETTING THERE
From Hāna, take Uaʻkea Road to just past the Hāna school (see area map, page 171 and site map, page 167). Parking is no longer allowed here along the road or in the small lot at the end, so backtrack to the nearest available legal parking. Then walk through the empty lot just south of the school.

About 2/3 of the way back in the lot, you'll find the start of the trail on the right. An interesting old Japanese cemetery will be on your left and the bay on your right. You will also see signs warning of danger on the trail. From this point, walk slowly to avoid slipping as you wind along the edge of the sea and eventually curve to the left where you'll find Red Sand Beach at the end of the trail.

Since the trail is deceptively slippery at all times and worse in the rain, take great care with children. No one should try to hike swiftly or close to the edge.

Note: when you get to the large tree with the "no trespassing" sign, take the trail to the right of the tree and follow the trail along the coastline, not very high up the hillside. If you hold left at the big tree, you will continue up a hillside past a lone last grave. This trail leads to a ridge where you can look down on Red Sand Beach. It's possible to climb down from here, but it's steep and dangerous and we don't recommend it.

Mel Malinowski

eyestripe surgeonfish (palani)

Hāna Bay

Hāna Bay offers excellent snorkeling, when conditions are calm. The best coral lies between the old pier and the light. We prefer to enter from the sandy beach and swim right under the pier to get to the snorkeling beyond. Explore the whole area beyond the pier, checking out the shallow spots close to the shore as well as wandering around the islands if it's calm enough there. We have seen groups of large turtles near the islands and lots of fish, coral and other critters in the protected cove just before the point.

In calm weather Hāna Bay is excellent for beginners to advanced snorkelers, offers easy entry, sandy beach, showers, restrooms, plenty of parking, and even some food when Tutu's snack bar is open. Those who would rather not swim far might enjoy a kayak tour. You'll find kayak rental and tours near the parking and Tutu's.

GETTING THERE

From the town of Hāna, take Keawa Place straight down to the harbor. Last time we were there, the sign was missing at the corner of Highway 36, so they may prefer the marked route on Uaʻkea Road instead. Park near the last shower on the right side of the bay. There you'll have an easy entry from the sandy beach and can swim to the best snorkeling. Alternatively, you can climb over some difficult rocks to get closer to the fish and coral right away, but it's far easier to swim.

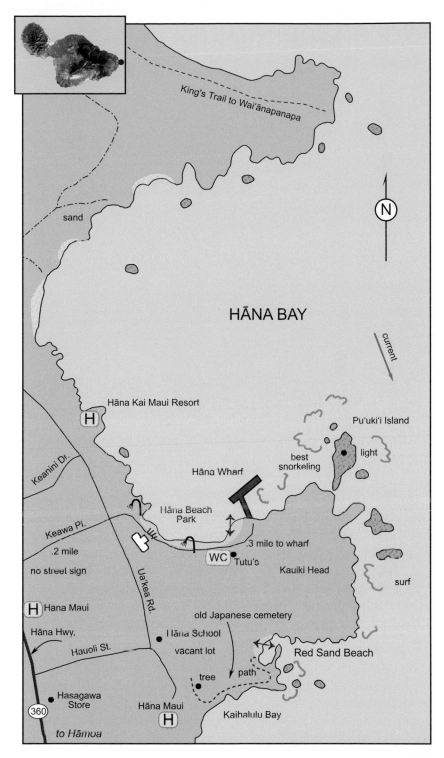

King's Trail to Wai'ānapanapa

sand

N

HĀNA BAY

current

Hāna Kai Maui Resort

H

Keanini Dr.

Keawa Pl.

.2 mile

no street sign

H Hana Maui

Hāna Hwy,

Hauoli St.

360

Hasagawa
Store

to Hāmoa

Ua'kea Rd.

Hāna Wharf

Hāna Beach
Park

WC Tutu's

Hāna School

vacant lot

tree

Hāna Maui

H

best
snorkeling

Pu'uki'i Island

light

.3 mile to wharf

Kauiki Head

surf

old Japanese cemetery

path

Red Sand Beach

Kaihalulu Bay

171

Wai'ānapanapa (Black Sand Beach)

Wai'ānapanapa State Park, just north of Hāna, is a beautiful place to camp with cabins, restrooms and showers available in a secluded location. Black Sand Beach (Pailoa Bay), within the park, is easy to find and worth the trip to picnic and enjoy the scenery.

It is often too rough for safe snorkeling. When calm enough, you can snorkel quite a ways to the right—even snorkel through a large natural arch. It's a pretty swim and you'll find some small coral and fish, but not nearly as much as Hāna Bay. The view of a huge rock arch from the water is spectacular, and the swim under it (if the tide is not high) is thrilling and dramatic. You'll know you're not in Kansas anymore. And at this beach, the sand is really, truly black.

Beginners can enjoy the beach, the view and a quick dip, while experienced snorkelers may want to try this for the novelty. Enjoy the beauty of the lava formations at this lovely park. You may also want to hike some of the King's Highway heading south along the coast—still within the state park. No showers near the beach, just several portapotties near the parking and plenty of shade.

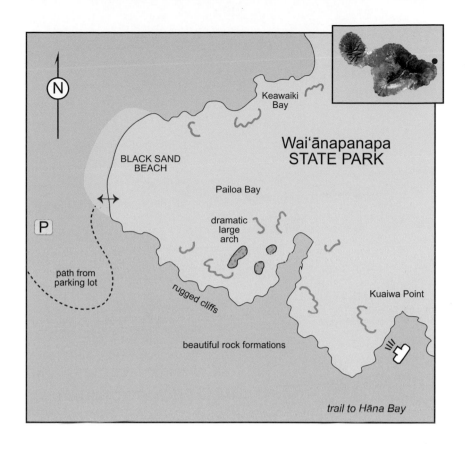

Keawaiki Bay

BLACK SAND BEACH

Wai‘ānapanapa
STATE PARK

Pailoa Bay

dramatic large arch

path from parking lot

P

rugged cliffs

Kuaiwa Point

beautiful rock formations

trail to Hāna Bay

N

GETTING THERE   The entrance to Waianapanapa State Park is located along the Hāna Highway (Highway 360) near mile marker 32 (see area map, page 159) and has a large sign mauka. The paved road with speed humps takes you straight toward the office at four tenths of a mile. At this junction (just before the office) the road to the right heads toward the cabins, while the one to the left heads to Black Sand Beach. Park at the end of the road where it overlooks the sea and you'll be able to look down to view Black Sands Beach. There are about a dozen spaces up here, but more nearby if it fills. Several portapotties are located on the left as you approach the end of the road.

To the right you'll see a paved path with steps down to the beach. The path takes you to the black sand beach where the inner cove is fairly well protected. Entry is easy in calm water, but stay out if you encounter waves. Snorkel within the outer points at all times. Watch the sea a bit from the parking area to determine how far is safe. You may want to stay within the big arched area.

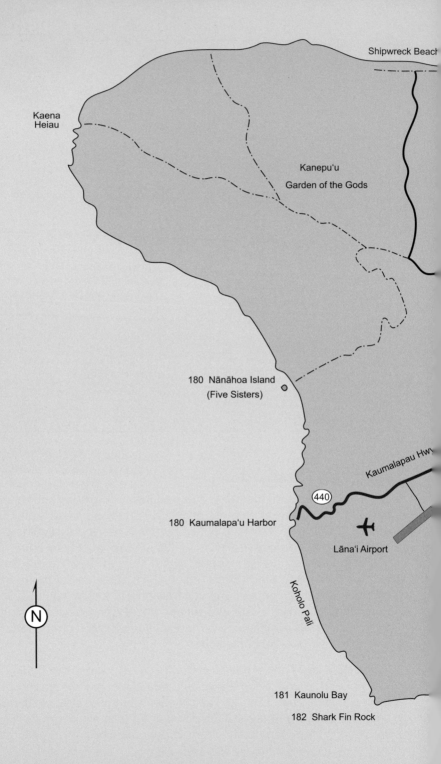

Shipwreck Beach

Kaena
Heiau

Kanepu'u

Garden of the Gods

180 Nānāhoa Island
(Five Sisters)

Kaumalapau Hwy

440

180 Kaumalapa'u Harbor

Lāna'i Airport

Koholo Pali

N

181 Kaunolu Bay

182 Shark Fin Rock

Snorkel Site Index Map

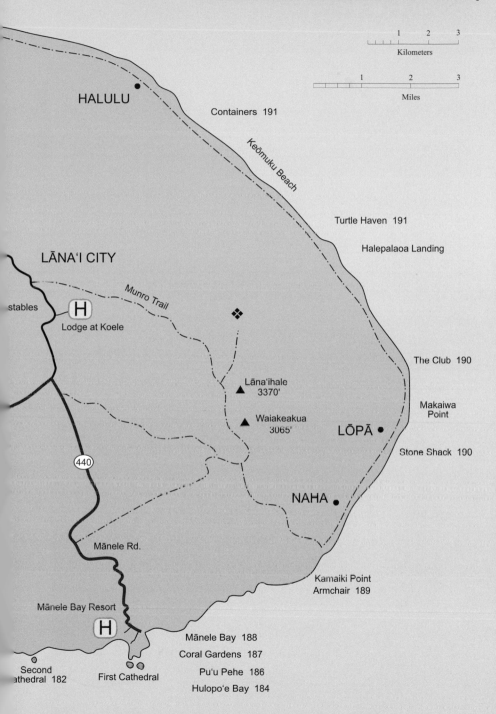

HALULU

Containers 191

Keōmuku Beach

Turtle Haven 191

Halepalaoa Landing

LĀNAʻI CITY

Munro Trail

stables

(H) Lodge at Koele

Lānaʻihale
3370'

Waiakeakua
3065'

LŌPĀ

The Club 190

Makaiwa
Point

Stone Shack 190

(440)

NAHA

Mānele Rd.

Kamaiki Point
Armchair 189

Mānele Bay Resort

(H)

Mānele Bay 188

Coral Gardens 187

Second
Cathedral 182

First Cathedral

Puʻu Pehe 186

Hulopoʻe Bay 184

1   2   3
Kilometers

1   2   3
Miles

Sites at a Glance

	Snorkeling	Entry	Sandy beach	Restroom	Showers	Picnic area	Scenic	Shade
Nānāhoa Island	B	1					•	
Kaumalapaʻu Harbor	B	1-2						
Kaunolu Bay	A	1					•	
Shark Fin Rock	A	1					•	
Cathedrals	A	1					•	
Hulopoʻe Bay	A	1-2	•	•	•	•	•	•
Puʻu Pehe (Shark Cove)	A	1-3	•				•	
Coral Gardens	A	1-2		•	•	•	•	•
Mānele Bay	A	2		•	•	•	•	•
Armchair	A	1	•				•	•
Lōpā (Stone Shack)	A	1	•				•	•
The Club	A	1	•		•	•	•	•
Turtle Haven	A	1					•	
Containers	A	1					•	

ornate butterflyfish

A	Excellent	1	Easy
B	Good	2	Moderate
C	Fair	3	Difficult

Page	Map page	
180	175	gorgeous site, not huge amounts of coral
180	181	some interesting, less common fish, near barge harbor
181	175	snorkel under towering cliffs, pretty spot, excellent
182	175	boulder habitat, deeper ocean, excellent snorkeling
182	175	under cliffs of S. Lānaʻi, boat only, room to explore
184	185	large beautiful bay, lots of coral channels
186	185	short hike from Hulopoʻe, tiny, but excellent if calm
187	185	excellent, secluded, short hike to facilities
188	185	tiny, varied fish near harbor, surprisingly good
189	175	extensive reef, best from boat, usually calm
190	175	best from boat, reef long & wide
190	175	extensive reef both ways, best from boat
191	175	from boat only, lots of turtles, extensive reef
191	175	from boat only, great reef, but often choppy

Mel Malinowski

saddleback butterflyfish

Lāna'i

For that one extra-special snorkeling experience, consider a day trip to Lāna'i, where beautiful Hulopo'e Bay awaits (see picture, page 184). A number of good snorkeling excursions make this trip daily from Lahaina Harbor, but you can also easily go on a self-guided trip by taking the ferry Expeditions. It leaves Lahaina Harbor four times a day, so take the early morning ferry, have coffee on the way, then spend a delightful day snorkeling several sites (Hulopo'e, Pu'u Pehe, and Coral Gardens)—all within a five-minute walk from Mānele Bay in Lāna'i. Stay for lunch and maybe even rent a car to tour the upper part of the island.

Two large beautiful resorts await if you want to stay longer. The Mānele Bay Resort (on Hulopo'e Bay) and the Lodge at Koele are both pricey, but excellent. The only other hotel option is a small hotel in Lāna'i City. The resorts have a frequent shuttle bus connecting them, so either will work for snorkelers.

Snorkeling is usually fairly uncrowded unless south swells are kicking up too much at Hulopo'e Bay. Then you might find all the snorkelers at Mānele Harbor. Boat trips have alternative destinations—most of which are listed in our sites. We've mentioned the popular spots even if they can't be reached from land. In the picture above you'll notice that Lāna'i has some VERY steep cliffs.

Hulopo'e Bay is the most popular and certainly the most scenic of these Lāna'i sites. It also has all amenities: long sandy beach, showers, restrooms, picnic tables, shade, drinking water, and a nearby hotel with excellent restaurants.

If you really want to snorkel to the fullest on your one day in Lāna'i, try to fit in Pu'u Pehe at the end of the trail (see map, page 185), and Coral Gardens back by the harbor. Although not as scenic or large as Hulopo'e, they both have plenty of interesting fish. Neither of these are best for beginners because entry can be a bit difficult.

Good showers and restrooms are available in the Hulopo'e Bay and Mānele Harbor area. All three of these sites need fairly calm swells from the south, so check the weather report before you come if you're intent on snorkeling in Lāna'i. The south swells are more likely in the summer when warm kona winds blow.

At any of these sites, stay away from the current beyond the far points. Hulopo'e Bay is plenty large enough to explore, so don't get tempted to head out where you might encounter a strong current.

Even small swells can make Hulopo'e a bit difficult for a beginner since you need to cross over an area with some chunks of rocks and coral. We advise holding your fins and walking out until you get to an area four or five feet deep (past where little waves slap against rocks), then it's easy to pull on your fins. This applies to the harbor area too because you want to step in carefully from the slippery rocks. Getting out is the reverse—just remember to take off those fins and toss them on the shore before you exit.

We've seen lobsters, parrotfish, a school of spinner dolphins, and most of the usual creatures. The coral in front of the hotel has a fair layer of algae, so it's not as pretty as it used to be, but fortunately the fish still abound.

Lāna'i has a long and broad reef along the east side, providing some good boat sites at times. Even where the cliffs are low, you won't want to snorkel from these beaches because it's difficult to cross the shallow part of the reef. Besides, they're too remote for safety unless a boat crew is at hand.

179

Nānāhoa Island (Five Sisters)

Five Sisters or Five Needles got its name from the five tall sea stacks or pinnacles located just south of the shore. One of the stacks fell during Hurricane 'Iwa in 1982. This is a gorgeous location on Lāna'i's far western shore, but has relatively small amounts of coral and fish. This is a perfect place to anchor for lunch and well worth the trip to see this lovely coast.

GETTING THERE   The only practical access here is by boat. It can be reached by the faster boats heading out from Lahaina. The zodiac-type boats have no problem circling Lāna'i when weather cooperates and you've chosen the longer trip.

Kaumalapau Harbor

Kaumalapau Harbor (also called Barge Harbor) is an unlikely-looking snorkeling site. It has interesting snorkeling, however, and offers some unusual fish including schools of pyramid butterflyfish. Don't go on a Thursday—the only day this big harbor is in full operation.

You'll find a small reef with fairly easy entry, clear water and lots to see. You do need to enter from rocks, slowly and carefully. Parking and crowds are certainly no problem here. Small waves break over the shallow reef in the center, making it look rougher than it really is. Swimming around the outside of the reef is usually easy and quite safe, but use care if swimming directly over such a shallow reef.

GETTING THERE   From Lāna'i City, take Highway 440 west to the harbor. Since Lāna'i has few roads, it's easy to find. Use the harbor parking lot and snorkel on the right side where you can see the reef from the lot. It's right next to shore. Enter to the left of the reef from the rocky shore and swim entirely around the small reef.

Hawai'ian cleaner wrasse

180

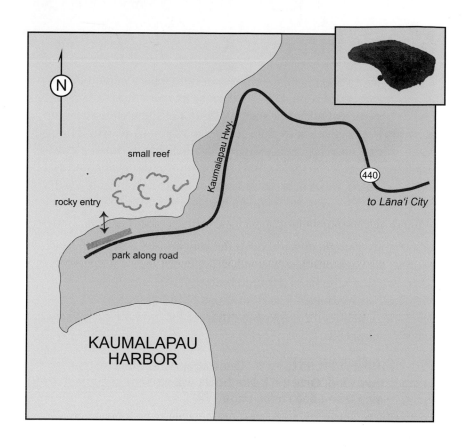

small reef

rocky entry

park along road

Kaumalapau Hwy.

(440)

to Lānaʻi City

KAUMALAPAU HARBOR

Kaunolu Bay

This usually calm, sheltered bay near the lighthouse in the southwest offers clear water with patches of reef and coral habitat. Most Lānaʻi sites are more exposed to open ocean, so Kaunolu Bay has an advantage when other sites are too choppy. There's a sandy bottom and mooring balls for several boats. Plenty of reef fish make this an excellent choice. Since it's right next to Shark Fin Rock, boats can easily take you to both.

GETTING THERE   There's no way you will be able to get to Kaunolu Point from the land. Fast excursions from Lahaina (see chapter about excursions) can zip over here for a day trip—especially the zodiac-type boats. These are the highest cliffs in Lānaʻi, so you won't find any kind of road down to the water.

Shark Fin Rock

This is a great snorkel and dive location right near Kaunolu Point. A very dramatic location, this site derives its name from a large rock in the shape of a shark's fin, sticking far out of the water. There are numerous little coves to explore for as far as you can swim. The coral isn't spectacular here (more of a boulder habitat), but plenty of fish hang out near the rocks. Most of the snorkeling is in about 10 to 20-foot-deep water near shore with some protection from swells. Watch carefully along the boulders because you may see octopuses and eels if you're patient.

When calm enough, do snorkel all the way around Shark Fin Rock because the back provides a wonderful view of the deep drop-off where we saw schools of pyramid butterflyfish—rarely seen in Maui's shallower water. The floor drops off quickly here providing a habitat for somewhat different fish and the dark blue water is delightful.

GETTING THERE   Once again, this site can't be reached from land. Only the faster boats will attempt to come this far from Lahaina (see Lāna'i map, page 174).

Cathedrals

Cathedrals sites are located along the cliffs of the southern shore of Lāna'i. Trilogy runs a small catamaran as an optional day trip for their Lāna'i excursion clients, and it's delightful. Scuba is often offered here as well. These days more excursions from Maui visit Cathedrals. A shelf of coral extends out from the cliffs at just the right height for snorkelers. You might be the only group of snorkelers in sight. Of course, if you are feeling brave and indestructible, you could jump in from the high cliffs as ancient Hawai'ians did. Getting out would be another matter!

GETTING THERE   This large site is for excursions only. Trilogy sometimes heads here from Mānele Bay, Ultimate Rafting from Lahaina, and several of the newer, faster boats. When south swell rolls in (more common during the summer), excursions are likely to head elsewhere because they don't you washing up on the base of the cliff.

182

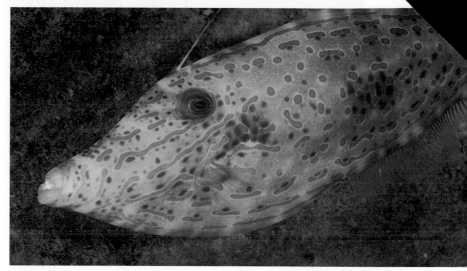
scrawled filefish

EXCELLENT

This large, beautiful bay in front of the Mānele Bay Resort is famous for good reasons. The lovely wide sand beach has showers, restrooms, drinking water, grass, and shade. Limited camping is allowed here, with a permit that must be obtained in Maui. This is one of the most dramatic beachside camping sites in Hawai'i.

When calm, you can snorkel anywhere, but don't miss the row of coral peninsulas jutting out like underwater ship piers over on the left all the way to the point. Cruise up the dramatic mini-canyons between them. We have seen big spiny lobster here in the daytime, as well as pelagic fish, parrotfish, raccoon butterflyfish, boxfish, many wrasses, eels and sometimes pods of spinner dolphins (as many as two hundred at once).

If surf is high (especially south swell), don't get caught between the waves and coral or rocks. We have seen a variety of weather in a few days—from calm as glass throughout the bay to large breakers. Keep in mind that all of the Lāna'i snorkeling sites face open ocean, so conditions vary depending on which way the swell is rolling. Even if surf is breaking, good swimmers can usually go beyond a small shorebreak, since the coral extends beyond the bay. Always stay

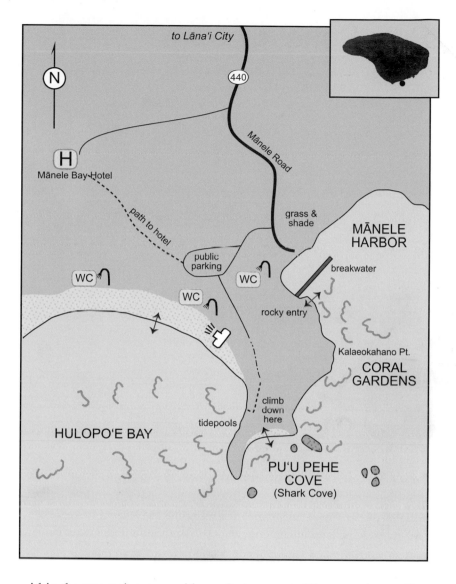

within the two points to avoid any fast currents. The water is usually fairly clear. A good part of the bay is about 10-20 feet deep. On the far left you'll see stairs coming down from the hill to tidepools, which are fun for kids. Do check the tide and surf conditions carefully first.

GETTING THERE
From the Mānele Bay Hotel, follow the path down to the beach and continue to the far left for the best snorkeling. From the Mānele Harbor it's a five-minute walk, but very sunny. Head out the exit road and take the first left.

Pu'u Pehe (Shark Cove)

Pu'u Pehe Cove is also called Shark Cove. If you don't mind climbing down a fifteen-foot cliff, which does have a crude trail, and is actually much easier than it looks, this bay has a pretty sandy beach and excellent snorkeling. No crowds down on this beach!

Pu'u Pehe Cove and adjacent Coral Gardens are our favorite shore-entry sites on Lāna'i. Entry is easy from the sandy beach, but only when calm. Snorkel to the left between the rocks, then continue as far as you like around the various rocks out to sea, unless you encounter currents near the far point.

As always, waves can vary in size and come from different directions, so conditions are quite changeable from day to day. Since this beach is fairly isolated in spite of being so close to a big hotel, don't snorkel here unless you feel sure that you can easily handle the ocean conditions. Of course, never snorkel alone at an isolated site like this. When the sea is calm, snorkel out through the shallow channel to the left and wander through Coral Gardens. We've seen plenty of fish, eels, and even octopuses up close.

When swell is too big, entry becomes dangerous in spite of the sandy beach, so don't try this one if you have doubts. Anyway, the water won't be very clear when waves are kicking up.

GETTING THERE   From Hulopoʻe Bay, walk out on the dirt road toward the far left point, past the stairs to the tidepools (see site map, page 185). Be sure to wear tennis shoes or reef shoes, hat and sunglasses since there's no shade. At the point we've marked on the map you'll find the only place to climb down the cliff on the far side. It helps if one person climbs down first and another passes them the gear. It's not as difficult as it looks, providing you go slowly and hold on carefully. There are no facilities here and no shade, but it's dramatic and worthwhile for swimmers and snorkelers. Serious snorkelers won't want to miss this one. All facilities are available at nearby Hulopoʻe Beach.

Coral Gardens

Just to the northeast of Puʻu Pehe, you can snorkel along the coast all the way to Mānele Harbor if it happens to be calm. Go slow and check to see if there's any current before heading out too far.

You'll find some good snorkeling along the rocky coast and patches of coral a bit further from shore. While there isn't a lot of coral, you'll usually find plenty of fish. This isn't for beginners because it can be quite choppy with some current. Besides, there won't be anyone around to help out if you get in trouble. When the water gets choppy, just snorkel the area near the harbor, but do watch out for boat traffic.

GETTING THERE   From the Mānele Bay Hotel, follow our instructions to Puʻu Pehe (see site map, page 185). As you enter the water make a left turn and snorkel between the rocks, then continue along the coast on your left.

From the Mānele Harbor, enter at the spot we have marked just south of the main Mānele Harbor. Take great care not to slip on the rocks as you enter. If conditions are calm enough, continue south along the coast—perhaps even ending up at Puʻu Pehe or Hulopoʻe Bay, where you can walk back to the harbor in five minutes.

nele Bay (The Harbor)

This appears at first glance to be an unlikely-looking place to snorkel. However, it has an excellent assortment of fish and coral for such a small site. Simply step off the boat or breakwater and snorkel in the little cove outside the breakwater, where you're away from harbor boat traffic. When calm, you can continue out toward the point or further out from the breakwater, where excursions often bring their snorkelers. If you enter from the rocky shore, be very careful not to slip on algae.

There's a grassy park next to the harbor with restrooms, indoor showers, drinking water, picnic tables and shade—everything except a beach. You could have a fine day trip right here. You'll probably have the little cove to yourself if it's early in the day. Explore along the breakwater, and weave in and out among the coral heads towards the point. In very calm weather, an expert snorkeler can swim all the way to Hulopoʻe Bay. Caution: it's a very long swim! When south swells roll in (especially during the summer) Hulopoʻe can be dangerous, so excursions then bring people to the harbor.

In the murky inner waters of the harbor itself, baby hammerhead sharks are sometimes seen. Boat traffic here is a little too busy for safe snorkeling in the inner area.

GETTING THERE From the Mānele Harbor dock, turn toward the tiny cove on the south side of the small breakwater (see site map, page 185). There's no beach, and entry is a bit tricky from the rocks at the north corner of the cove. See the map for entry point. Wear shoes even though it's a short distance because the rocks can be slippery, sharp and sometimes hot. Entry is from the rocks, so take great care not to slip on algae.

You'll wonder why you're here until you duck your head underwater. If you encounter a current or large swells, stay within this sheltered area. If calm, you can snorkel out and along the coast to the right— not to the left into boat traffic. Beginners should not try this entry, but can snorkel this area from a boat entry. Even when choppy, there lots to see, so experienced snorkelers are likely to love it.

Alternatively, you can enter the water from the dock and swim quickly to the right around the breakwater—watching out for boat traffic and looking for those baby sharks at the same time. This is also a good alternative exit route in case swells pick up while you're having fun.

Armchair (Kamaiki Point)

Armchair has a pinnacle about 75 yards offshore, where you will find fish and coral near the top. This is a popular dive site. Snorkelers need help finding the spot, so it's best to arrive by boat. It isn't always a safe place to snorkel since swell and currents can be a problem at this exposed southeastern site.

GETTING THERE Though possible by land, access is better by boat with a captain to show you where it is. Besides, waves are often rolling in along the whole eastern side of Lāna'i. The snorkeling area is well beyond the waves, but can be choppy enough to make it better for diving than snorkeling. While this site can often be calmer and safer than those further north, it's still vulnerable to open ocean conditions. You'll want to snorkel here only when visibility is good.

Mel Malinowski

male parrotfish

189

Lōpā (Stone Shack)

This extensive snorkeling site (also called Stone Shack or Fish Shack) is at the southern end of Lāna'i's seven-mile long reef. You can wander up and down this broad reef, always staying away from the waves breaking against the shore. The reef extends to the shore, but boats anchor well beyond the waves. Most of this reef is ten to twenty feet beneath the surface, so it helps to have good visibility.

Some patches of reef may seem to have few fish, but keep snorkeling and you're bound to come across big groups of fish as well as plenty of turtles. This is usually the calmest spot along Lāna'i's long eastern reef. Summer swells can ruin the visibility.

GETTING THERE   This site is best accessed by day-trip boat. They can place you well beyond any danger from waves hitting the shore. The captain can assess the best conditions and visibility along this extensive reef. Shore access is possible, but should be left to experienced local snorkelers because it usually involves a swim over coral and through waves (see map, page 174).

The Club

This section of Lāna'i's largest reef is directly in front of a privately-owned eight-acre chunk of land where Club Lāna'i used to take its excursions. The future of the land is unsure, but the reef in front is still in good condition, although it does have some algae problems. The Club folks called it the best-preserved reef in Hawai'i. While we like it, we wouldn't rate it that high. It is extensive.

Like Stone Shack to the south, The Club (also called Club Lāna'i or Coral Gardens) offers broad reef extending in both directions and is a popular excursion destination. Most of the reef is about 10-20 feet deep. While the fish aren't concentrated in one spot, you can wander through a broad area and see plenty of coral, fish and turtles.

GETTING THERE   This is a popular site with excursions from Maui because there's plenty to see and they can easily find sandy areas to anchor without damaging the coral. Entry from land is not available at the moment and would be hazardous due to the waves over coral close to shore. There is a nice, sandy beach with very shallow water—perfect for small children if and when it's available again.

190

Turtle Haven (Twin Palms)

Heading north from The Club following this long reef you'll find Turtle Haven (often called Twin Palms). While the tall palms on the beach mark this site, there are several other pairs of palms along this coast so you probably wouldn't find it on your own. This site is within the seven-mile long reef and has a natural bowl in the coral where turtles like to hang out. With them will be tangs who like to eat algae off the turtles' shells. The coral here is beautiful and has channels of sand running perpendicular to shore.

GETTING THERE   Beach access is only available to experienced locals on this remote northeastern coast of Lānaʻi. Boats from Lahaina make the trip when conditions are good. When swells from the north kick in, they'll look further to the southern part of this reef for calmer conditions.

Containers

This northernmost site on the seven-mile long reef is named for the shipping container seen on the beach. The coral here is unusually beautiful. This northeast location means relatively few days of calm seas. When the trade winds start to blow from the northeast (75% of the time), you'll need to head south to snorkel. This is not a common destination for excursions.

GETTING THERE   Too remote for beach access, you'll have to come by boat on one of the excursions out of Lahaina. Only the faster boats are likely to come this far and only with good conditions, so this isn't a site you can count on. Trust your captain to decide if it's a good choice.

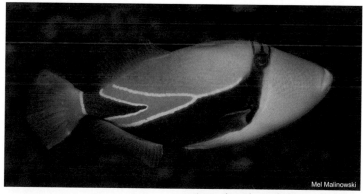

Mel Malinowski

rectangular triggerfish

191

Moloka'i

"The Friendly Isle" of Moloka'i is easily accessable from Maui by way of ferry or plane, and from Oahu via a 30 minute flight. Some people pop over for the day to see the highlights, but you might want to consider staying to explore the other sights, and do some snorkeling, too. You can drive the length of Moloka'i in about two hours! Conditions here are often more difficult and changeable than Maui, but the outer reef sites are pristine. The north shore catches big waves and current much of the time, so snorkeling is usually only practical in the south. The south side of Moloka'i has a thirty-mile long reef in excellent condition, but access is difficult from the shore (up to two miles out!). Boat based snorkeling is your best bet.

Tim Forsberg at Moloka'i Fish & Dive (fishanddive@mobettah. net) takes snorkelers to various sites offshore as conditions allow. You need to be an early riser: most trips leave by 7 a.m. His trips go early because the wind-driven swells build up early, often by 10 a.m. The outer reef is broad, with lots of colorful coral (bright blue, pink, yellow, purple and green) in excellent condition. The fish populations here tend to be small, perhaps due to overfishing, but there's plenty of variety. In the shallow inner lagoon we have seen a fuchsia flatworm, large turtles, snowflake moray, and lots of reef fish.

For skilled and adventurous snorkelers, there are a few shore-entry spots. All require great care due to rips, currents and tides. Halawa Beach Park (picture on page 192) at the far east end of the highway is well worth a visit for the dramatic views, but is usually not safe for snorkeling. The east end beach at mile marker 20 3/4 is pictured above, with mixed coral and rocks; it's worth a look, but is often much too rough. A bit further to the west is Murphey's Beach at mile 20, which is OK, but only when the tide is quite high. Our picture below shows it at low tide to give you an idea just how low it can go. This is what much of the south inner reef looks like at low tide!

Traveling along the main east-west highway all the way to the end brings you to Kapukahehu Beach (often called Dixie Maru Beach) at the far western end of the paved road (pictured above). This simple but pretty cove is well-protected from all but severe winter storms, and offers pleasant swimming and picnicking as well as a bit of snorkeling. There is not much coral, but you can see some fairly large fish on the far right and left sides near the rocks.

This is the calmest and safest of the west end beaches, where you will find five marked beach access right of ways, with small parking lots along the road to Dixie Maru—all with a simple shower near the parking. They all look appealing, but study them carefully for some time, as the arrival of a large wave set can close them out in just a few minutes time. Keep this in mind if you enter from rocks.

This whole west coast is dramatic, but prone to rips and currents, as well as heavy swell, so only inner Dixie Maru is usually safe enough for beginners. There are many times when nothing else here should be attempted.

Lovely, long Papohaku Beach is pictured below, where a wave like this one can arrive at any time and grind you on the rocky bottom. Not recommended for beginners and rarely even for advanced swimmers and snorkelers. Papohaku Park is spacious and has picnic tables, lots of kiawe shade trees, and restrooms with inside showers, although they weren't too clean when we were there.

Moloka'i Island remains quiet, uncrowded and very friendly. They seem to have no desire for a flood of tourists. You won't find a McDonalds or Costco here, nor many timeshare condos. Enjoy the greenery, varied vistas and pristine outer reef without any crowds. Accomodations are mostly quite simple condos, or the rather pricey Moloka'i Ranch Lodge accomodations (unless you have access to one of the multi-million dollar beachfront estates springing up along the west end). The highways have two lanes, sometimes narrowing to only one, business hours can be short (especially on Sunday), restaurants are few, and nightlife is hard to find. If these modest amenities don't satisfy, perhaps you're better off in the more mainstream life on Maui. Moloka'i offers a unique low-key experience like the Hawai'i of many years ago.

Please be respectful and show aloha here. Take the time to drive the full length of Moloka'i to see the spectacular and lush Halawa Valley in the east, the miles of ancient fishponds along the south shore, dramatic Kalaupapa National Park and the dry, but beautiful west end.

Marine Life

The coral reef supports tremendous diversity in a small space. On a healthy reef, you've never seen everything, because of the boggling variety of species, as well as changes from day to day and changes from day to night. The reef functions much like the oasis in the desert providing food (more abundant than the open ocean) and shelter from predators. Only the wild rain forests can compare with the reef in complexity.

In Hawai'i the coral reef itself is less spectacular than in warmer waters of the world. This is counterbalanced by the colorful and abundant fish, which provide quite a show.

There are excellent color fish identification cards available in bookstores and dive shops. We particularly like the ones published by Natural World Press. There are also many good marine life books that give far more detailed descriptions of each creature than we attempt in these brief notes.

OCTOPUS

Some varieties of octopuses hide during the day while others hunt by day. They eat shrimp, fish, crabs, and mollusks—you should eat so well! Octopuses have strong beaks and can bite humans, so it's safer to not handle them.

Hawai'ian day octopus

Being mollusks without shells, they must rely on speed, cunning and camouflage to escape danger. Octopuses are capable of imitating a flashing sign, or changing their color and texture to match their surroundings in an instant. This makes them very hard to spot, even when they're hiding in plain sight—usually on the

Hawai'ian night octopus

bottom or on rocks. They can squirt ink to confuse predators. They only live about two years.

Just because you haven't seen one does not mean they aren't there. Go slow and watch carefully for a rock or coral that moves. It may take you some time to find one (weeks? months?) but when you do, it is a real thrill.

SHRIMP

In all kinds, colors, and sizes, they like to hide in rocks and coral—often living symbiotically with the coral. They are difficult to spot during the daytime, but at night you will notice lots of tiny pairs of eyes reflected in the flashlight beam. Most are fairly small and well-disguised.

banded coral shrimp

Some examples include: the harlequin shrimp (brightly colored) that eat sea stars, the banded coral shrimp (found all over the world), and numerous tiny shrimp that you won't see without magnification.

SEA URCHINS

Concealed tube feet allow urchins to move around in their hunt for algae. The collector urchin has pebbles and bits of coral attached for camouflage. These urchins are quite common in Hawai'i, and have no hazardous spines.

Beware of purple-black urchins with long spines. These are common in shallow water at many beaches. It's not the long spines that get you, it's the razor-sharp ones hidden beneath. The bright red pencil sea urchin is common and easy to spot. Although large, its spines aren't nearly sharp enough to be a problem for people. The spines can actually be used for chalk.

banded sea urchin

SEA STARS

brittle star

Abundant, but not seen much by snorkelers. The crown-of-thorns sea star, which has venomous spines, is found in Hawai'i, but not in large numbers like the South Pacific. Sea stars firmly grasp their prey with strong suction cups, and then eat at their leisure.

RAYS

Manta rays (large plankton-eaters) use two flaps to guide plankton

manta ray

into their huge efficient mouths. Mantas often grow to be two meters from wing-tip to wing-tip, and can weigh 300 pounds. They can't sting, and are a real treat to watch.

Mantas feed at night by doing forward rolls in the water with mouths wide open. Lights will attract plankton which appeal to the manta rays. Dive boats can attract manta rays with their bright lights making the night trips to see these creatures very exciting.

Another beautiful ray, the spotted eagle ray, can sometimes be seen cruising the bottom for food and can grow to be seven feet across. They have a dark back with lots of small white dots and an extremely long tail. Their fins function more like wings so they seem to be

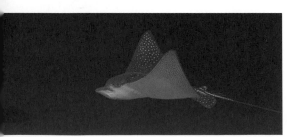

spotted eagle ray

flying along rather than swimming.

Common sting rays prefer the sandy bottom and usually stay in calm, shallow, warmer water, where they can evade people.

198

EELS

Many types of moray eels abound among the reefs of Hawai'i. Some can grow to two meters long. While you may not see any on a given day, you can be sure they are all around the reef hiding in crevices.

whitemouth moray eel

Varieties of moray found in Hawai'i include undulated, whitemouth, snowflake, zebra (black and white stripes), wavy-lined, mottled, and dragon moray (often reddish-brown with distinct white spots of differing sizes).

Morays prefer to hide in holes during the day. If out cruising, they often find a nearby hole when spotting a snorkeler. When they stick out their heads and breathe, their teeth are most impressive.

undulated moray eel

Eels generally have no interest in eating snorkelers, other than very pushy and annoying ones, while they are quite able to swallow a fairly large fish. Please avoid putting your hands into reef crevices, since this is a great way to spend the afternoon getting stitches.

TRUMPETFISH

These long, skinny fish can change color, often bright yellow, light green with shaded bars, or light blue—and will change color in front of your eyes. They sometimes hang upright to blend with their

environment, lying in wait to suck in their prey. They also shadow other fish and change their color to sneak up on prey—even at a cleaning station.

They do eat throughout the day, which is unusual for fish-eaters, who usually eat at dawn or dusk.

trumpetfish

Trumpetfish are quite common in Hawai'i and often seen hanging out alone. Some grow to more than one meter long, although you will usually see only the smaller ones.

Cornetfish are similar to trumpetfish in shape and size, but have a distinctive thin filament extending from the center of the tail. Sometimes small cornetfish can be seen in big groups. Adults can be larger than trumpetfish and can also change color.

cornetfish

NEEDLEFISH

These pointed, common silvery-blue fish like swimming very near the surface, usually in schools—occasionally leaping from the water. All types of needlefish are long and skinny as their name implies, and grow to as much as two feet long. Color and markings vary, but the long narrow shape is distinctive and hard to mistake. They're usually bluish on top, and translucent below for camouflage.

BUTTERFLYFISH

Butterflyfish are beautiful, colorful, abundant and varied in Hawai'i. They have incredible coloration, typically bright yellow, white, orange, black, and sometimes a little blue or red. They hang out near coral, eating algae, sponges, tube worms and very small coral polyps.

ornate butterflyfish

No one really understands the purpose of their beautiful colors, but many have speculated. Perhaps they serve territorial or mating needs.

threadfin butterflyfish

Juveniles are often distinctly different in coloring. Bizarre patterns may confuse predators—especially since they can pivot fast. Bars may help some hide, while stripes are seen more in faster fish. Black lines across the eyes and spots near the tail may also confuse predators.

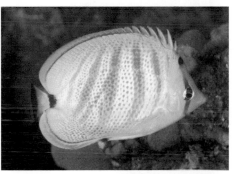
multiband butterflyfish

Butterflyfish are often seen in pairs remaining together for up to three years. They're all delightful to watch. Hovering and turning are more important to them than speed since they stay near shelter of the reef and catch a quick meal—like a tube worm.

longnose butterflyfish

201

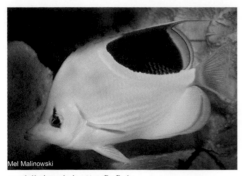

Mel Malinowski

saddleback butterflyfish

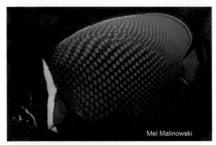

Mel Malinowski

reticulated butterflyfish

fourspot butterflyfish

teardrop butterflyfish

The ones you are most likely to see while snorkeling in Hawai'i include: raccoon (reminding you of the face of the animal), ornate (with bright orange lines making it easy to spot), threadfin (with diagonal lines), saddleback (fairly rare), lemon (very tiny), bluestripe (a beautiful one found only in Hawai'i), fourspot, milletseed, teardrop, and forceps (also called longnose).

The lined butterflyfish is the largest variety found in Hawai'i. The reticulated, often found in the surge zone, are not common, but are particularly beautiful. The smaller ovals (found in pairs scattered around on most reefs) seem to glow from within, especially on a sunny day.

Many butterflyfish have black spots across the eyes and near the tail—perhaps to confuse a predator about which way they're headed. Watch and they may confuse you too.

Most butterflyfish are common near the reef and pay little attention to snorkelers so they're fun to watch and often easy to identify with their distinctive markings.

202

PARROTFISH

Among the most dramatically colored fish on the reef, male parrotfish are blue, green, turquoise, yellow, lavender, and/or orange with endless variations of these colors. Females tend to be a more drab reddish brown. No two are alike. Parrotfish are very beautiful, with artistic, abstract markings.

female parrotfish

These fish change colors at different times in their lives and can also change sex as needed. They can be quite large (up to one meter).

Mel Malinowski

male parrotfish

Patient grazers, they spend countless hours scraping algae from dead coral with their large, beak-like teeth, and create tons of white sand in the process. Most prefer to zoom away from snorkelers, but you'll see them passing gracefully by and will hear them crunching away at the coral. Unfortunately they are heavily fished, so less numerous lately.

Mel Malinowski

Picasso (lagoon) triggerfish

TRIGGERFISH

Fond of sea urchins as a main course, triggerfish graze during the day on algae, worms and other small items.

Varieties include the Picasso (wildly colorful—quite rare at many sites, but worth watching for), reef (the Hawai'ian state fish), pinktail (easy to identify with its black body, white fins and pink tail), black (common, distinctive white lines between body and fins). The checkerboard triggerfish has a pink tail, yellow-edged fins, and blue stripes on its face. Triggerfish are beautiful and fascinating to watch.

lei triggerfish

Mel Malinowski
pinktail triggerfish

scrawled filefish

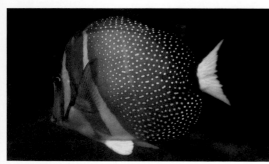
spotted surgeonfish

Mel Malinowski
goldring surgeonfish

204

FILEFISH

The scrawled filefish has blue scribbles and brown dots over its olive green body. Quite large, up to one meter, often in pairs, but seen occasionally in groups.

A filefish will often turn its body flat to your view, and raise its top spine in order to impress you. This lets you have a great close-up view — and a perfect photo opportunity.

SURGEONFISH

Razor-sharp fin-like spines on each side of the tail are the hallmark of this fish, quite common in Hawai'i. These spines provide excellent defense, but aren't needed to fend off tourists since surgeonfish can easily swim away.

Varieties includes the orangeband surgeonfish (with distinctive long, bright orange marks on the side), as well as the pretty blue Achilles tang, which has large bright orange spots surrounding the spines near the orange tail. The common yellow tang is completely yellow and smaller. The sailfin tang has dramatic vertical markings. It's less common, but easy to identify.

WRASSES

Wrasses are amazingly bright and multicolored fish. Hawai'ian cleaner wrasses set themselves up for business and operate cleaning stations, where they clean much larger fish without having to worry about becoming dinner. They eat parasites, and provide an improbable reef service in the process. Perhaps their bright colors serve as neon signs to advertise their services. Hang out near their cleaning stations for excellent fish viewing. In Hawai'i, the tiny cleaner wrasse (about two inches) is neon yellow, purple-blue and black.

eyestripe surgeonfish

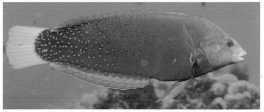
yellowtail coris

saddle wrasse

Other wrasses are larger including the dazzling yellowtail (up to 15 inches), which is covered with glowing blue spots, many stripes, and a bright yellow tail. The juvenile yellowtail is bright orange with a few big white spots, looking completely different from the adult.

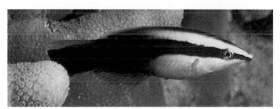
Hawai'ian cleaner wrasse

The saddle wrasse is endemic to Hawai'i. It is bright blue, with green, orange and white markings. Wrasses are closely related to parrotfish, but usually smaller.

male bird wrasse

205

SCORPIONFISH

The Hawaiʻian lionfish (sometimes called a turkeyfish) is very colorful example, with feather-like multicolored spines. Beware of their poisonous spines, though! Don't even think about touching a scorpionfish, and try to avoid accidentally stepping on one.

Hawaiʻian turkeyfish

Other scorpionfish are so well-camouflaged that they are hard to see. They just lurk on the bottom blending in well with the sand and coral. If you see one, count yourself lucky, but don't step on it!

PUFFERFISH

Pufferfish (and the related trunkfish) swim slowly due to their

male spotted toby

boxy shape, so need more protection. Puffers can blow up like prickly balloons when threatened.

Two kinds are common in sheltered areas: porcupine (displaying spines when inflated), and spotted trunkfish, boxfish and tobies (often brown or black with lots of white dots). Most tend to prefer to escape under the coral, although some seem unafraid of snorkelers and even curious. You may spot a big porcupine face peering out from under coral (giving the appearance of a much larger fish such as a shark).

The small spotted toby is common over the reef. The female is brown

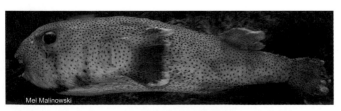

with white spots and the male is a beautiful dark blue with orange spots.

porcupinefish

SHARKS

Although sharks have quite a reputation for teeth rather than brains, they are unquestionably survivors, having been around for about 300 million years.

This is an extremely successful species with keen hearing, smell, sight and ability to detect electrical signals through the

blacktip reefshark

water. They swim with a side-to-side motion, which does not make them speedy by ocean standards.

When snorkeling you are unlikely to spot any shark except the whitetip or blacktip hanging around shallow water. Plenty of larger species pass by Hawai'i, but tend to travel the deeper waters further out in the channels.

DOLPHINS

Spinner dolphins are frequently seen in large schools (at least 200). They swim as small family groups within these schools, and often swim fast, leaping out of the water to spin in the air. They tend to hang out in certain locations, so you can search for them if you like.

spinner dolphin

spinner dolphins

Spinners are a bit sleeker than other dolphins and arrive at large bays to rest during the day. Dolphins sleep on one side at a time, so they can swim while resting.

207

Bottlenose dolphins often approach fast-moving boats, and it is a great thrill to watch them race along just in front of the bow of your boat, jumping in and out of the water with grace and easy speed.

Beaked and spotted dolphins are also commonly seen in the waters off Hawai'i.

bottlenose dolphins

SEA TURTLES

Green sea turtles (the most common in Hawai'i) are becoming more plentiful lately and seem to be less concerned about snorkelers.

Sea turtles are often seen in pairs. Larger specimens (often seen along the southwest shore) can be up to 100 years old, and tend to be docile and unafraid. You'll often see them resting on the bottom in about ten to twenty feet of water during the day. They sometimes let you swim as close as you like, but it's best to avoid hovering over them because they do need to come up for air. Just before dusk, they often hunt for algae along the lava coastline and don't seem to mind being tumbled against the sharp rocky shore.

Do not disturb these graceful creatures, so they can remain unafraid to swim among snorkelers. In Hawai'i it is against the law to touch or harass sea turtles. Enjoy, but don't crowd them.

green sea turtle

WHALES

Humpback whales migrate here to breed in winter, around December through early April. Humpbacks come quite close to the coast, and are most numerous in February. They are so large that you can often easily see them spouting and breaching. Their great size never fails to impress, as does their fluid, seemingly effortless graceful movement in the water. Many excursions offer whale-watching trips during the winter season. Listen for the whales when you snorkel.

NOAA

NOAA

humpback whales

Weather

All islands have a windward side, which is wetter, and a leeward side which is drier. In Hawai'i, the northeast is windward and hence wet, and the southwest is leeward, or kona, and hence drier and sunnier. Waves from afar tend to arrive from the north in winter and from the south in summer, although big swell can arrive from any direction at just about any time of year.

Hawai'i gets most of its rain in the winter. The most severe storms (called kona) come from the south and can even bring hurricanes in the summer. Temperatures tend to be very mild year-round, yet there is variety around Maui on any day of the year. There are days when you could tan in Wailea in the morning, drive up to cold Haleakalā later, while warm rain continues in Hāna. Summer temperatures are five to eight degrees F warmer than winter.

Evaporating moisture from the ocean forms clouds. As the clouds rise over the mountains, they cool, and the condensing moisture becomes rain. Hāna receives about 130 inches of rain a year, while Lahaina is so dry at times that it is reputed to have derived its name from a Hawai'ian word meaning "cruel sun".

Having lost most of their moisture in passing over the mountains, the clouds have little left for the leeward side—so it is in the rain shadow of the mountains. The leeward weather is therefore often sunny. Waikīkī, Po'ipū, Kā'anapali, and Kona are all in rain shadows. On Maui, if you get stuck with heavy rains in Hāna or Kapalua, just head for Kīhei or Mākena, and you're likely to find the sun.

Changeable is the word for Maui's weather—not just between areas, but also rapidly changeable in any given place. The trade winds blow about 90% of the time in the summer and about 50% in the winter. They tend to be stronger in the afternoon and are stronger in Kīhei where they are funneled between the mountains.

The windward or northeastern coasts have much more rain, wind and waves—something important to remember when snorkeling. The most dependable and pleasant snorkeling in Hawai'i is on the Kona side. Yet, there are occasional times during the year when calm conditions on the windward side allow access to enjoyable snorkeling areas there. If the odds of good conditions are just too small, we don't review these areas.

Seasonal Changes

Hawai'i has much milder weather than the continental United States, yet it is has seasons you might call winter, spring and summer. At

210

20°N Latitude, there are nearly 2 1/2 hours more sun in midsummer than in midwinter, which is 21% more. But the moderating effect of the ocean keeps temperature swings quite moderate.

Winter is the cooler, wetter season. Cooler is a relative term, as the average high temperature in winter falls to a brisk 80° F, as opposed to a summer average high of 86° F. Low temperatures on Maui may dip as low as 60 degrees, but more commonly are not below the high 60s even in winter.

Water temperature in winter falls to around 75° F, and at times, wind, rain and cooler air temperatures can temper your desire to splash around in the water. Winter usually begins in mid-November, with the start of winter storms from the north-northwest. This is the start of the large wave season on the north coast. Winter tails off in mid-March.

Spring really is just the transition from winter to summer, and is marked by the end of winter storms in mid-March. Hours of sunshine go up, especially on the west, leeward side of the island. This can be a very pleasant time of year. Spring transitions into summer in May.

Summer begins in May, as the weather warms, and the rains slacken. Trade winds temper the heat and humidity almost all the time. This is prime sunning and play time. An occasional tropical storm or hurricane can come through, and swells can roll in from the south. The heat softens in October as summer draws to an end.

Water Temperature

On the surface, the water in Hawai'i gets as low as 75° F in March to as high as 80° F (27° C) in September. Sheltered bays can be a bit warmer, while deeper or rough water can be surprisingly cool. Kaua'i, being furthest north of the main islands, is typically a little cooler than the other main islands. If you happen to be slender, no longer young, or from a moderate climate, this can seem cooler than you might like—especially if you like to snorkel for hours.

Hurricane

Summer is possible hurricane season, but it is also the time when weather is typically excellent. While the storms don't last long, they can be terribly destructive. Hurricanes can bring amazingly heavy rain and winds to the islands. Any could receive a direct hit, which happened when Hurricanes 'Iwa (1982) and later much stronger 'Iniki (see page 87) clobbered Kaua'i. Fortunately very few hurricanes ever actually hit Hawai'i directly.

Month by Month

JANUARY   This month offers an opportunity for the wettest weather all year. It's also one of the coolest. Large surf can often pound the north and west exposed beaches of Hawai'i.

FEBRUARY   Just as cool, the surf continues to hit the north and west exposed beaches, although storms are a bit less frequent than January. Occasionally, there will be a week when the wind and swell drop, the visibility clears, and snorkeling and diving conditions are superb. There is no way to predict when this will occur, however.

MARCH   The weather starts to improve with fewer storms, especially in the west.

APRIL   Spring arrives early, so warm weather begins during this month. Expect a few late swells, but also more calm, beautiful periods.

MAY   Summer is already arriving—especially in the south and west. This tends to be a trouble-free month. Mid to late May is one of our favorite snorkeling times, and few tourists are around, so you can feel like you have Maui to yourself.

JUNE   This offers very warm and dry weather with plenty of sun. Fortunately the winds blow nearly every day. Early June is usually great snorkeling weather, and the crowds have not arrived.

JULY   Much the same as June, except that storms in the South Pacific begin at this time. They hit beaches exposed to the south (called south swell).

AUGUST   Another warm month, occasional big waves can hit the southern exposed beaches (more south swell).

SEPTEMBER   This last month of summer can sometimes be the hottest and most humid. Hurricanes can strike Hawai'i, and are most common this month. Most will miss the islands, but bring muggy weather. 'Iniki, however, brought widespread damage to Kaua'i. Maui has seldom been seriously affected. This can be a great month in the water. It can also be exceptionally rainy in east Moloka'i this month and next.

OCTOBER   Milder weather begins this month with the start of
            storms arriving from the north.

NOVEMBER   The first real winter storms arrive this month, and
            they can be somewhat cool. Since they stir up the
            water, visibility usually goes down.

DECEMBER   This is winter with frequent storms and wind
            bringing big waves to the exposed northern and
            western beaches. However, even this month can be
            clear and warm between storms.

Coolest month:	February
Hottest month:	September
Rainiest month:	January
Driest month:	June
Coolest water:	December-April
Warmest water:	August-September

Tsunami

Huge waves can be triggered by earthquakes either in the islands
or far across the Pacific. Though quite rare, separated by decades
usually, they've hit Hawai'i a number of times, more often from
the north. Depending on the exact direction, they can directly hit a
valley and really wipe it out and rinse it clean. It is better to not be
there when this happens. Groups of tsunami waves are spaced about
fifteen to twenty minutes apart, and often catch unsuspecting folks
who go down to the beach too soon.

There's likely to be plenty of warning due to ever-vigilant earthquake
monitoring equipment, elaborate modeling systems, and large
numbers of beach-side tsunami warning sirens. Authorities prefer
to warn of every possible tsunami just to be safe. It doesn't pay
to ignore warnings just because the sea appears calm. If a major
earthquake strikes while you're visiting, it's a good idea to head
rapidly for high ground. Leave bays or valleys which can act to
funnel the effects of a large wave.

Due the superior forecasting and warning systems now in place,
Hawai'i is unlikely to ever experience the unforewarned destruction
of the huge Indonesian tsunami of December 26, 2004. To help
insure that this is so, if you hear a loud warning siren, and don't have
very good reason to know it is just a test, play it safe and leave the
beach immediately for high ground.

213

Language

English is now the official language of the islands of Hawai'i (except for the island of Ni'ihau.) However, most place names and lots of slang are Hawai'ian, so it's helpful to at least be able to pronounce enough to be understood. It's a very straight-forward phonetic language: each letter is usually pronounced just one way. The long place names aren't nearly so daunting when you have learned the system.

All syllables end with a vowel. When the missionaries attempted to write this oral language, they used only seven consonants (h,k,l,m,n,p,w). However, there is actually an eighth consonant in spoken Hawai'ian, the glottal stop (called an 'okina)—marked by the '. This is not the same as an apostrophe: ' .When you say 'Uh-oh' in American English, you are using a glottal stop.

Five vowels (a,e,i,o,u) were used by the missionaries, but there are actually five more, the same vowels pronounced with a longer glide and more stress: ā, ē, ī, ō, and ū. A horizontal line (called a kahakō) is placed over these vowels. Nēnē, for example, is pronounced like "Nehh-Nehh" with a little 'a' in there, soft. We have attempted to include all kahakōs (macrons) and 'okinas, so it will be easier for our readers to pronounce the words properly. Researching proper place names is a challenge, as some of the proper spellings and meanings are being lost. If we have made mistakes, we hope our more knowledgeable Hawai'ian readers will understand and let us know for future editions.

Each and every letter is pronounced in Hawai'ian, except for a few vowel combinations. However, locals often shorten names a bit, so listen carefully to the way natives pronounce a name.

Another addition to the language is a form of pidgin, which served to ease the difficulties of having multiple languages spoken. Laborers were brought in speaking Japanese, Mandarin, Cantonese, Portuguese, English, as well as other languages, and they had to be able to work together. Pidgin evolved as an improvised, but surprisingly effective way to communicate, and much of it survives in slang and common usage today. It's very interesting to hear and learn, but we'd suggest you be very circumspect about using it unless you study it carefully. It can sound affected from the mouth of a tourist, possibly coming off as if you're mimicing and disrespecting locals. It may be better to just listen and enjoy the lilt.

Pronunciation

Consonants are pronounced the same as in English, except that the W sounds more like a V when it appears in the middle of a word.

Unstressed vowels are pronounced as follows:

a = *a* in *a*bove
e = *e* in b*e*t
i = *y* in cit*y*
o = *o* in s*o*le (without off glide)
u = *oo* in m*oo*n (without off glide)

Stressed vowels are a little different, and none have off glides:

a or ā = *a* in f*a*r
e = *e* in b*e*t
ē = between 'ehh' and *ay* in p*ay* *(not quite that hard)*
i or ī = *ee* in s*ee*
o or ō = *o* in s*o*le
u or ū = *oo* in m*oo*n

When pairs of vowels are joined (as they often are), pronounce each, with slightly more emphasis on the first one. This varies somewhat with local usage. It is beyond the scope of this book to teach the complexities of spoken Hawai'ian, but maybe we'll get you started.

Learning to respect and pronounce some Hawai'ian will bring you closer to the heart of the Hawai'ian culture. Our goal is to make you aware enough that you can understand what you are hearing, and not be daunted by the many beautiful, but multisyllabic words.

Kealakekua, for example, is not so hard: it has four syllables: Ke.ala. ke.kua and means: Ke (The) ala (pathway) (of) ke (the) kua (gods). Now you're ready for humuhumunukunukuāpua'a (the state fish of Hawai'i): humu.humu.nuku.nuku.āpu.a'a. See, it's easy once you divide it up!

After you get the hang of it, you may come to feel, as we have, that Hawai'ian is one of the most mellifluous languages on earth. This may be part of the reasons songs in Hawai'ian have become popular far beyond the islands. Modern folksingers such as Iz (Israel Kamakawiwa'ole) and Keali'i Reichel have contributed by writing and singing beautiful new songs in Hawai'ian. Listening to their new as well as traditional songs is a great way to learn the pronunciation of this delightful language!

Often Heard Myths

- *"You'll probably never see a shark."*

  If you snorkel often, you probably will see one occasionally, but a reef shark, not a great white or tiger shark. Reef sharks prefer seafood for dinner. If you look at actual statistics, your time is better spent worrying about lightning or pig attacks.

- *"Barracudas are harmless to humans."*

  Perhaps some are quite innocuous, but others have bitten off fingers or hands. The great barracuda has been involved in the few cases we've read about, mostly involving fishing. Don't worry about one that has been hanging out in front of a hotel for years, but you may not want to crowd them either. I'd be more worried about eating one for dinner, because they are a definite, major cause of ciguatera "fish poisoning". They are one tasty fish, though, in our experience. Feeling lucky?

- *"Jewelry attracts barracuda bites."*

  I first heard this rumor from a 12-year-old, and it was later reinforced by numerous books. The idea is that the flash will fool a barracuda into attacking. However, we've never verified a definite case of a person losing an ear lobe this way, even though I see people swimming and diving with earrings all the time. The same goes for wedding bands. I keep mine on and haven't had a problem.

- *"The water in Hawai'i is too cold for comfort."*
  "The water is Hawai'i is as warm as bath water."

  It can be pretty cool, especially late winter, especially if you go in naked (see *Basics*); but there is an alternative. Just wear a thin wetsuit and it will feel a lot like the Caribbean. Or you can wait till late summer and give the water a chance to warm up. Don't expect warm water (particularly in Kaua'i, in the winter months).

- *"It rains all the time in Maui."*
  "Maui is too hot and sunny."
  "It's always windy in Maui."

  In Maui you can have the climate of your choice. Don't believe everything you read in advertising literature (like hotel brochures) regarding perfect weather. It does vary, there are seasons, and location matters. It just depends on your personal preferences. You may hit a patch of rain, but it seldom lasts for long (though it can rain all week in the north at times!). The typical weather report for Wailea is Tonight — fair; Tomorrow, mostly sunny; for the weekend, sunny except for some upslope clouds in the afternoon. The drama of weather is part of the charm of the tropics — enjoy it as it is, rather than expecting it to be exactly as you want.

- *"Octopuses only come out at night."*

  Some types are nocturnal, some not. We've seen lots in Hawai'i quite active during the day. The hard part is spotting them! Pay your dues, look sharp, and you'll see one eventually. Shallow beaches with rubble are excellent places to spot octopuses.

- *"Maui is getting too crowded and commercial."*

  While there is certainly no problem buying a T-shirt in town or finding sun-worshippers on the beaches, there are plenty of spectacular sites to snorkel that are completely uncrowded. As long as you have a car, it's easy to drive to delightful and secluded locations — usually within half an hour from your hotel or condo. Hiking on Maui can take you completely away from civilization as you know it, but a good map (such as ours) can lead you to some lovely snorkeling sites as well as romantic vistas to enjoy the sunset and the view of neighboring islands. And for really getting away from it all, try a ferry trip to quiet Lāna'i or even quieter Moloka'i.

Index

Activity Warehouse 97
'Āhihi Bay 150
  map 147
'Āhihi Cove 146
  map 147
'Āhihi-Kīna'u
  Natural Reserve 152
  map 153
'Alaeloa 69
  map 63
aquarium in Mā'alaea
  map 103
Aquarium 155
  map 153
arc-eye hawkfish 87
Armchair 189
authors 224
Azeka I & II
  Shopping Center 101

banded coral shrimp 197
banded sea urchin 197
bandit angelfish 167
banyan tree 68
Barge Harbor 180
  map 181
barracuda 31
basics 8
Benadryl 21
Big Beach 142
  map 135
bird wrasse 143, 205
Black Rock 74
  map 75
Black Sand Beach
  (Makena) 138
  map 139

Black Sand Beach
  (Hana) 172
  map 173
body suit 14
booties 14
bottlenose dolphin 208
boxfish 206
brittle sea star 198
butterflyfish 201

Cape Kīna'u 153
caring for your gear 24
Cathedrals 182
Cemetery 78
  map 79
Chang's Beach 124
  map 125
Charley Young Beach Park 104
  map 101
cleaner wrasse 180, 205
clearing your mask 22
The Club 190
cone shells 34
Containers 191
convict tang 18
Coral Gardens (Lāna'i) 187
  map 185
Coral Gardens (Maui) 98
  map 91
cornetfish 69, 200
correction lenses 10
Cove Park 104
  map 101

defog for masks 19
discounts 97
disposable cameras 123
dive boats 161
Dixie Maru Beach 194

Doctor my Eyes 49
Dolphin Plaza 101
dolphins 207
D T Fleming Park 58
  map 59
drowning 34

East Maui Area 158
  map 159
eels 33, 199
eyestripe surgeonfish
  22, 169, 205
Expeditions ferry 82, 178

filefish 204
fins 12
Fish Pond 152
  map 153
Five Graves/Caves 126
  map 127
Five Sisters 180
Four Seasons Resort 111
fourspot butterflyfish 202

gear selection 9
goldring surgeonfish 204
Grand Wailea Resort 111
great barracuda 31
green sea turtle 151, 208

Halawa Beach Park 193
Hāmoa Bay 162
  map 163
Hāna Airport 159
Hāna Bay 170
  map 171
Hāna Highway 159
Hāna Wharf 171
Hanakaōʻō Beach Park 78
  map 79

Hasagawa General Store 151
hawkfish 87
hazards 26
Hekili Point 93
  map 95
Hoapili (King's) Trail 153
Honokahua Bay 58
  map 59
Honokeana Bay 68
  map 63
Honokōhau Bay 48
  map 47
Honokōwai Beach Park 70
Honolua Bay 52
  map 53, 57
Honolua-Mokuleʻia Bay
  Marine Life Conservation
  District 53
Hotel Hāna Maui 159
Hulopoʻe Bay 184
  map 185
humpback whale 209
hurricanes 211
Hyatt Regency Kaʻanapali 77
hypothermia 29

If You Love the Reef 117
Ironwoods 58
  map 59

Jodo Mission 85

Kāʻanapali Aliʻi 77
Kāʻanapali Beach 76
  map 77
Kahana Beach 61
Kahekili Beach Park 72
  map 73
Kahului Airport 5

Kalama Beach Park 104
    map 101
Kalepolepo Park 101
kama'āina rate 97
Kamaiki Point 189
Kama'ole I 105
    map 101
Kama'ole II 106
    map 101
Kama'ole III 106
    map 101
Kanahena Beach 144
    map 135
Kanaio Coast 157
    map 153
Kapalua Bay 64
    map 63
Kapalua Bay Resort 63
Kapalua West Maui Airport 4
Kapukahelu Beach 194
Kaumalapa'u Harbor 180
    map 181
Kaunolu Bay 181
Kea Lani Resort 111
Keawakapu Beach Park 108
    map 109
Keawala'i Bay 129
    map 127
Keawala'i Church 127
Keka'a Point 74
    map 75
Kenoehelele'e Bay 51
Kīhei Area 100
    map 101
Kīhei Boat Ramp 107
    map 101
Kīhei Surfside 109
Koki Beach 164
    map 163

Lahaina Area 82
    map 83
Lahaina Cannery Mall 85
Lahaina Center 83
Lahaina Harbor map 88
Lahaina Shores 83
Lahaina Visitor Center 83
Lāna'i 178
    map 174
Lāna'i Airport 174
Lāna'i Sights at a Glance 176
language 214
La Pérouse Bay 156
    map 153
Launiupoko Wayside 92
    map 91
Leho'ula Beach 163
lei triggerfish 203
lionfish 33, 206
Little Beach 140
    map 135
The Lodge at Koele 175
longnose butterflyfish 201
Long's Center 101
Lōpā 190
low volume mask 17

Mā'alaea Harbor 102
    map 103
Mai Poina 'oe La'u Park 101
Mākena Bay 127
Mākena Landing 128
    map 127
Mākena State Park 135
Mākena Surf condos 124
    map 125
Māla Wharf 84
    map 85
Maluaka Beach 136
    map 137

Mana Kai Resort 109
Mānele Bay Harbor 188
  map 185
Mānele Bay Resort 185
manta rays 32, 198
map symbols 45
marine life 196
Marriott Maui 77, 111
mask 10
mask cleaning 24
mask straps 12
Maui road map 4
Maui Kā'anapali Villas 73
Maui Ocean Center 102
  map 103
Maui Prince Hotel 136
  map 137
Maui snorkeling sites 36
Meclizine 21
Mile 14 94
  map 95
Mōkapu Beach 112
  map 111
Mokulē'ia Bay 56
  map 57
Moloka'i 192
Molokini Island 130
  map 131
Moorish idol 11
moray eels 33, 199
motion sickness 21
multiband butterflyfish 54, 201
Munro Trail 174
Murphey's Beach 193
mustaches 11
myths 216

Nākālele Point 48
  map 47

Nāmalu Bay 62
  map 63
Nānāhoa Island 180

Nāpili Bay 66
  map 63
Nāpili Kai Beach Club 63
Nāpili Plaza 63
Nāpili Point Resort 63
Nāpili Point Shopping
  Center 63
Nāpili Sunset 63
needlefish 200
North Maui Area 44
  map 45

octopus 85, 196
'Oheo Gulch 159
Old Airport Beach 72
  map 73
Old Lahaina Shopping Center
  83
Olowalu Area 90
  map 91
Olowalu General Store 91
Olowalu Wharf 95
Oneloa Bay 58
  map 59
Oneloa Beach 142
  map 135
Onuoli Beach 138
  map 137
ornate butterflyfish 176, 201
Outrigger Wailea 111

pacing 23
Pailoa Bay 173
Palauea Beach Park 120
  map 119
Pali tunnel 91

Pāpalaua Wayside 98
    map 91
Papohaku Beach 195
parrotfish 189, 203
peacock flounder 165
peacock grouper 24
Picasso triggerfish 137, 203
pinktail triggerfish 202
Pioneer Inn 83
Pioneer Sugar Mill 83
poisonous fish 33
Polo Beach 118
    map 119
Polo Beach Club 119
Poʻolenalena Beach Park 122
    map 119
Portuguese man-of-war 31
pronunciation 214
psychedelic wrasse 129
Puamana Beach Park 89
    map 83
pufferfish 206
purge valve 10
Puʻu ʻOlaʻi Beach 140
    map 135
Puʻu Pehe Cove 186
    map 185

raccoon butterflyfish 103
Rainbow Mall 101
rainfall 210
rays 32, 198
rectangular triggerfish 191
Red Sand Beach 166
    map 167
reef shark 35
reef shoes 14
reef squid 91
Renaissance 111
Residences at Kapalua 63

reticulated butterflyfish 202
rip currents 28
Ritz Carlton 59
rockmover wrasse 121
saddleback butterflyfish
    177, 202
scorpionfish 206
scrawled filefish 183, 204
scuba 161
seasickness 21
sea jellies 31
sea star 198
sea turtles 208
sea urchins 30, 197
Seven Pools 159
Shark Cove 186
    map 185
Shark Fin Rock 182
sharks 35, 207
Sheraton Maui 77
Shipwreck Beach 174
The Shops at Wailea 111
shrimp 197
sign language 25
Slaughterhouse Beach 56
    map 57
snorkel 9
Snorkel Gear Rental 145
snorkel holder 9
snorkeling site map
    Lānaʻi 178
    Maui 38
Snorkeling Sites at a Glance
    Lānaʻi 176
    Maui 40
snorkeling vest 16
Snuba 71
South Maui Area 134
    map 135
spinner dolphin 207

spotted boxfish 206
spotted dolphin 207
spotted eagle ray 198
spotted surgeonfish 149, 204
sting ray 198
Stone Shack 190
Stouffer's Grand Wailea 111
Sugar Beach Resort 101
Sugarcane Railroad Station 83
squid 91
sunburn 26
surface diving gear 17
surgeonfish 204
swim cap 16

teardrop butterflyfish 202
temperature 211
threadfin butterflyfish 201
triggerfish 203
trumpetfish 200
tsunamis 213
turtle 151, 208
Turtle Haven 191

Ukumehame Beach Park 98
    map 91
Ulua Beach Park 114
    map 111
Understanding Waves 27
underwater cameras 123

Wai'ānapanapa State Park 172
    map 173
Waihikuli Wayside Park 80
    map 79
Wailea Area 110
    map 111
Wailea Beach 116
    map 111
Wailea 'Elua 111

Wailua Falls 159
Waiohuli Beach 101
water temperature 211
waves 27
weather 210
West Maui Airport 4
West Maui Area 60
    map 61
Westin Kā'anapali 77
Westin Villas 73
wetsuit 15
Whaler's Village 77
whales 209
whitemouth moray eel 33
White Rock Beach 119
Windmill 50
    map 51
wrasses 121, 143, 161, 205

yellowtail coris 51, 205

About the Authors

Judy and Mel Malinowski love to snorkel in the warm oceans of the tropics.

This love has led them to embark on snorkeling and cultural adventures to 70-some countries from Anguilla to Zanzibar. Hawai'i kept drawing them back, infusing their lives with aloha and teaching respect for the 'āina.

Although they are certified scuba divers, the lightness and freedom of snorkeling keeps it their favorite recreation. Whenever possible, they are in the water every morning by 7 a.m.

Mel, Judy and their three children have hosted students and cultural exchange visitors from Bosnia, Brazil, China, Germany, Nepal, New Zealand, Serbia, and Turkey in their home, and helped hundreds of other families enrich their lives through cultural exchange.

Working with exchange students and traveling as much as their businesses allow has encouraged their interest in the study of languages from Mandarin Chinese to Hawai'ian. They are graduates of Stanford University.

Mel and Judy live on the South Kohala coast of the island of Hawai'i.